BORN TO LIVE

LIVE

FOREVER IN BLACK

BORN TO LIVE

LIVE

FOREVER IN BLACK

DAVE MONTANNA

Daisa
PUBLISHING

First published in Great Britain in 2023 by
DAISA PUBLISHING
An imprint of PARTNERSHIP PUBLISHING

ISBN 978-1-915200-44-0

A CIP catalogue record for this book is available from the British Library.

Book typeset by:
PARTNERSHIP PUBLISHING
North Lincolnshire, United Kingdom

www.partnershippublishing.co.uk
Printed in England

Partnership Publishing is committed to a sustainable future for our business, our
readers, and our planet; an organisation dedicated to promoting responsible
management of forest resources. This book is made from paper certified by the
Forestry Stewardship Council (FSC) an organisation dedicated to promoting
responsible management of forest resources.

We operate a distinctive and ethical publishing philosophy in all areas of our
business, from our global network of Authors to production
and worldwide distribution.

DEDICATION

A special tribute to my Mum and Dad, without them this story wouldn't have been possible.

I remember them with much love and affection.

BORN TO LIVE

FOREVER IN BLACK

This is my life story, and I can share the title means something special to me. I often find myself dressed in...

'BLACK' as a Football Referee.

'BLACK' whilst on stage doing my Roy Orbison tributes, (Roy pretty much always wore black) and personally trying to keep in the 'BLACK' (financially) throughout my life, which at times has been such a challenge.

I wouldn't say this is an autobiography as such. True, it is about me, but it's just as much about my family and the characters I've met during my lifetime. During the Pandemic, my family asked me to write down some of my memories – starting from the very beginning. I did hesitate for a while, but finally decided, if it was for them and not for me, then I should go ahead. Which it is what I have finally done.

I am a deadline sort of person and by keeping the flame 'alive' I can move quickly. I need to plan that 'Yes, one day this will happen', otherwise I will probably find something else to put my life and soul into.

So far, it is working well.

Another main reason for continuing this adventure, was a 'chance' and inspirational, meet - one evening after a theatre show I was working at, with the director of a book publishing company no less, who was waiting in the foyer at the time and just by speaking to each other for a few minutes – our conversation turned to books, and we registered a certain reason to meet up again. I willingly took her calling card and that was the only motivation I needed to seize this new opportunity to share my story.

I do hope you find my story as interesting, exciting, and inspirational as I have living and writing it. I always have strived to go 'beyond the fringe' and tell it all as it was.

So, sit back, relax and enjoy as you read my journey... 'Born to Live ~ Forever in Black'.

FOREWORD

Dave Montanna born 'David Orriss' is the first son of Kitty and Frederick Orriss who lived most of their life in Lee Street, Kingston-Upon-Hull. My aunty Kitty and uncle Fred were, without doubt, two of the nicest and kindest people who have inhabited this planet. David was born soon after WW2, on 5th August 1946.

My parents weren't so lucky as I was born at just the beginning of that war, but I was too young to notice the extreme difficulties living in what was one of the most bombed cities in England.

Like me David knew nothing of sweets, oranges, bananas... growing up in the 40's and early part of the 50's. Our mothers used to meet often so I grew up having young David as a friend, often meeting in East Park, Hull. The friendship continued and sometimes included some of my friends until eventually I left schooling in 1958 and moved away from Hull. David, however, has remained steadfastly committed to Hull and a keen supporter of Hull City AFC, and has led a successful life entertaining the citizens Kingston-Upon-Hull, the UK and pretty much worldwide as a striking sound and lookalike to Roy Orbison in the many tribute shows on land and at sea.

David was encouraged to play guitar by my most talented and musical father, Stan, for which I know David is forever thankful.

Finally, I fully support David in his quest to write about his life, because he too, is one of life's gentleman, big hearted and altruistic, - like his mum and dad!

Geoff Todd

A doctor was talking to a lawyer at a party...

"I've often wondered why when people find out I'm a doctor do they ask me about their health problems?"

"Well," replied the lawyer, *"I have the same issue. They ask me about legal issues."*

"So how do you respond to that?" asked the doctor.

"I just send them an invoice for services rendered," said the lawyer.

"What a great idea," said the doctor.

The next day the doctor received a bill from the lawyer!

CHAPTER ONE
BORN TO LIVE!

I came out alive and breathing thankfully, but unusually breach which is of course 'headfirst', in the front bedroom of 218 Lee Street, Hull. 'My new home' is one of the longest streets in our area, if not in all of Hull itself.

Growing up was always a happy time, and I remember quite vividly, as a four-year-old, playing with the pots and pans after mum had finished washing and drying them. It's strange, but almost impossible to know you are around in your early year's, memory wise. But 'hey ho', we lived at the bottom end of the street, which was a cul-de-sac, meaning as a developing child I had lots of room to play outside with others, and without the worry of traffic (vehicles were basically still a new innovation).

We had various weekly visitors such as: the horse and cart selling fruit and vegetables, the lemonade man from Laws, and a milk delivery which was by a hand 'propelled' cart. No motorised or electronic devices during that period. At that time although the area across the street is now a school, but previously while I was still quite young, the area was barren, and some neighbours referred to it as a the 'farm' which I was led to believe it was at one time.

From Left: Brother Howard, Mum, Dad, & Me

As a child I had a good upbringing, dad worked locally at Reckitt & Sons Limited, and I would wait at the corner of our street and Chamberlain Gardens for him to appear each weekday lunchtime. I would get a ride on a small seat he had affixed to his cycle crossbar for the short ride back to our house.

I can vividly recall my Aunty Pat and Uncle Stan came to pick mum, dad, and me up for what I thought was a Sunday afternoon ride in this new-fangled way of transportation... a car!

Dad, Auntie Elsie, Mum, Pat, Stan
& Geoff

My thoughts were completely shattered however as we stopped at the Victoria Children's hospital. I was taken in by mum and dad and told I would be staying in to have a tonsils procedure. This was the end of my world, and I sobbed forever. However, the procedure was to my good fortune, as it appeared that by year six, I found that I had a boy soprano voice! (I always blamed this on my operation to remove my tonsils) Later on in my vocal development I was chosen as a student to sing at the famed 'Hull City Hall' during the annual Christmas concert but I would be singing

SOLO! Even at that age I was made up, but equally nervous. "Nothing wrong with that," said my music teacher. "Just enjoy the experience!" Now to rewind a few years or so...

My first morning at Cavendish Primary school as an infant passed, and at lunchtime I came home. Mum asked, 'What was your morning at school like?' I remember to this day what I said.

"Well it was alright, but I don't think I will go back again!"

Words of wisdom or maybe fortitude? Needless to say, I gave up on that one while I was losing. So, return to school is what I had no choice but to do!

My brother Howard was born in 1953 and our childhood together was very enjoyable, even though the 7-year difference in age was apparent. At such a young age the gap can be huge, but we got along great, still do today. I introduced him to football, cricket, and other sports.

We spent many a happy hour on the school field, which was opposite to where we lived.

My Dad though, thought I would never get an interest in football, so as an 8-year-old he took me to see my first football game between Hull City and Blackburn Rovers. We lost 1-4, with Syd Gerrie scoring for us, and I was smitten for life! I joined our school team and quickly learned the basic rudiments of the beautiful game.

My dad was always a massive influence in my upbringing. As a joiner he made many different things for my use, such as: a wooden steam engine that as a youngster I could sit in, a pogo-stick which was very popular with all the kids in the neighbourhood, a 'Bogie' which was all the rage as a young lad. (For the uninitiated a 'Bogie' is a four wheel sit on contraption that could be pushed, or better still, went fast on a downhill movement. Lots of fun and many kids owned one.) It is funny how habits change due to progress.

For instance, I spent many an hour with my local neighbourhood friends playing football on the school field opposite to our house. We never had bottles or cans (that were not yet invented), so if we needed a drink, we dashed home over the school gates and ran home the 100 yards or so. Gulped as many cups of water we could, then returned back to the footy game.

In the past times it was not possible to carry a drinks dispenser that anyone could carry to have a drink out of as this receptacle was yet to be invented! Funny old world then!

Such a simple technique but it had not been thought of. We played with the neighbours' children in the summer months at cricket and arranged matches between local street teams. I asked my dad to make me a wooden shaft to enable me to mark out a cricket pitch with proper whitening. I always liked to attempt reality in everything I did whenever possible. We played with marbles another past pastime. Another was in conker season dipping them in vinegar to harden them before we put them on a string and then batter the life out of your opponent's conker to try and win that round.

Dad was so influential throughout my early and teen years, and we were very close, in that he was always interested in what I was doing and how my life was developing.

Mum too was a lovely person who enriched both mine and Howard's development as youngsters growing up. Dad was always so practical in his approach whereas I had no interest, nor did I like doing practical things like woodwork, hand work of any kind, apart from using my Pen and Pencil!

Dad, Brother Howard & Mum

As a family we frequently visited Aunty Pat (real name Martha but she much preferred her aka name as Pat). Aunty Pat was a big influence on my development. She and I were very close, with lots of advice on savings and life in general. My uncle Stan who was a teacher at a local secondary school also came in very handy to help me with my Technical Drawing homework. I was really dire at this subject and also woodwork of which my uncle taught also.

He was rather upset when I let him do my homework and my school tech drawing tutor only gave him 3/10! Uncle Stan said he should go and see my tutor, but I talked him out of it by saying that I thought he was an alright teacher (well I had to consider he was my football coach at school as well!) At the time I had this typewriter and I managed to convince my Uncle Stan to buy it off me for the princely sum of £14. I had spotted a guitar on sale -brand new for £17 in Woods music shop in Hepworth Arcade in the Hull's old town. The pound notes still stuck to my hand, and with the assistance of a further £3 from mum I bought my first instrument. I was barely 16 years at the time, and I hadn't much of a clue how to negotiate this lovely instrument. In conversation my dad said that a great guitarist was resident at the local Ace of Clubs social club which was just around the corner from where we lived, his name was Jack Meddings, who really was an exceptional guitarist- he almost made it talk!

Ace of Clubs, Hull

Well, dad was convinced if he put cash in Jack's hand, would he come and give me some lessons? Jack agreed and although he was a very pleasant guy who lived by himself, he would always arrive at teatime and mum would always feed and water him first and then I would get down to learn how to control this amazing instrument.

Jack was really influential in my development, but Jack being Jack would sometimes come late, sometimes he never turned up at all. Other times he arrived unexpected, and really in the end he became such a lovely friend to us all. Mum often packed him up with some supper, as I think she felt a little sorry for him. Eventually after some time, Jack left the local club he was working at and moved across to do a summer season in Jersey. (A wonderful place that played a big part in my musical and promoting future which you will read later).

I convinced my dad to stand as guarantor to allow me to purchase my VOX AC 30-watt amplifier which cost the princely sum of £150. I had the payment book and as I had to pay out of my wages a monthly instalment until the balance became nil. Wish I had hung on to that amplifier as they now sell for a figure in excess of £1500!!

CHAPTER TWO
GET YOUR PROGRAMMES HERE!

During my early teenage years, I also became interested in collecting Football Programmes and memorabilia. This probably came about through my schoolfriend David Bell who had a small collection. I knew David from about nine years of age, as we lived close by and I also knew his Uncle Billy, who rode everywhere on his bike, and we often used to say hello to him as he passed by.

I often took a bus into town and walked down Spring Bank, one of Hull's oldest roads, when another contact, (I cannot recall who) told me about this shop that sold football programmes. It was a bit of a 'bric-a-brac' retail establishment really. My visits to that shop inspired me to continue to pursue this growing hobby and I do remember that they had a basket with mainly Halifax town programmes. I collected and swopped with my pal David. His Uncle Billy was an ex-football referee and he seemed to be able to receive invites to see top matches at that time. With these games came a host of programmes that he had brought home and given to his nephew David. We often swopped items to start our collections. As a fourteen-year-old I read Charles Buchan's Football Monthly and became aware of a page featuring swop programmes/sell section. I must have drove my mum mad as I sent postal orders and received parcels of programmes regularly, with some badly packed, (maybe as this was a new innovation) which must have drove the local post office 'potty'.

Over a period of years when I stopped collecting (but it was always in my mind to continue this at some point) my mum unbeknown to me had stored all my collections in the loft. One day when I was about 17, I asked mum where my programmes were stored? She immediately said she had given them all to a Boy Scout troop. Make no mistake I was gutted, not only gutted but livid. I needed to start all over again! Why, oh why, do parents have a spring clean every year? I had always intended one day to re kindle my football programmes interest. At this time many dealers in football merchandise were beginning to surface and I started to build a good collection which I have since, never ever, let go of really. I wonder why? I began to go back to the business side of things and bought often in a wholesale manner. For instance, I dealt direct with Wembley and on one occasion I drove down in 1984 to pick up 500 copies of the 1984 cup final Programme Watford v Everton.

I was lucky enough to meet a boyhood hero of mine David Stacey, who was a very big name in Football Programmes as a dealer, who was visiting Wembley himself to collect some FA Cup Final Programmes. In fact when I lived at Hull Road, Cottingham and sometime later in the year he stopped overnight with us after a fair I had organised at the Central Methodist Hall in

Hull, which was next door to one of my newsagent retail outlets.

We were lucky enough to have Radio Humberside attend to interview myself and some of the other stallholders that day, with comments broadcast live describing all the information about the Fair. The next day after breakfast we were onto our next Programme fair being held at Sincil Bank the home of Lincoln City AFC.

Back to the 1984 F.A. Cup Final programmes and the week before the final match took place, I stood outside Hull City's Boothferry Park ground pre match and sold every one of the 500 copies to the fans on their walk up to the last league match of the season. People remarked how can you have the official match programme a week before the event? I said just a bit of shrewd business.

I have from an early age had an eye for making a buck or two!

One guy bought 5 copies and this steam rolled. At 2:50pm, from 12pm, I had sold out! Also, in my future days as a self-employed newsagent (1980-1996) I sold many copies of forthcoming matches, such as European Cup finals, European Cup, Winners Cup Finals, FA Cup Final issues, and so on over the next few years. I did in fact also organise a number of football Programme Fairs in Hull and took a regular stall at St. Luke's Church Hall at Everton AFC. This was the best fair I ever went to and reasonably regular too. In those days I would take between £2-250 during each fair I attended during the mid-eighties but would lose about £30 in 'nicked' items. Liverpool citizens did not take kindly to purchasing in the normal way. That said I still made more profit even allowing for the stolen items.

I used to leave my car on a piece of waste ground on these regular Scouse forays. One day a young lad said, "If you give me a fiver, I will look after your car until you come back for it, after the game has finished." I did think that was a good idea as Walton was not a particularly safe area of Liverpool at that time. Just parking on nearby waste ground.

I carried on with this arrangement for several journeys, then I thought, 'I have an Alsatian dog of my own by the name of Fritz, so why don't I take him with me and save paying this same young lad a fiver!' Well, I duly arrived that early Saturday morning ready for the programme fair. The very same young lad came up and said, "Usual deal mister?"

I said, "Well no, I have got my dog to look after the car."

The lad thought for a minute then he said, "Well can your dog put fires out Mister?"

I thought for a minute or so... then said, "Ok, point taken," and he kept his job!

At that time too I had become a good friend of Bobby Brown, who at that time, was involved looking after the Hull City football junior team. Bobby, a Londoner, was an England amateur international centre forward who 'scored goals for fun'. Well, that's how most people described him. A lovely man, his family lived in Newport just outside of Hull. Bobby also was involved in the management days of Mike Smith, Chris Chilton, and has the distinction by a winning percentage of being the most successful manager in Hull City's history.

Bobby eventually moved to South Wales. I missed seeing Bobby when he came to the new KC stadium a few years back, and only found out after the game he had been literally yards from me without me knowing, when he attended a match at the stadium. My dad was quite taken up with Bobby, and on an occasion or two I would call with Bobby at my mum and dad's house for a cuppa and a good natter, which my dad loved to do.

I managed to attend trips to Programme Fairs at Lincoln, York, Peterborough, Tranmere, Blackburn, Leeds, and so many others. These were often on a Saturday and Sunday, and it helped the business grow very quickly. I spent time with a lovely pal namely Bill Chester, who was an avid football programme collector, but nowadays more of a photo signature collector.

We often went to a Hull City games and I recall a trip to see the Tigers at Burnley (a win by 3-0 would see us promoted, but we only won 2-0.) Great days in the eighties that's for sure. I see Bill occasionally to this day at the MKM Stadium, where he collects mainly autographs rather than programmes. Bill was so devoted to collecting programmes that, as a bricky by trade, he redid some work for me at the Hull Road address and wanted paying only in programmes and not cash! What an amazing and lovely fellow Bill is.

In later years, I attended many auctions at Christies, Sotheby's in London, Sportingold, Sporting Memory's, and many more UK wide. Only three years ago I organised an auction myself, utilising Baitson's auctioneers in Hull. Michael Baitson had been almost a lifelong friend from my late teens and his son Andrew helped' me set up a really big football Programme and Memorabilia auction, which was in one of the newly timed auctions.

They work on a similar way to a normal auction, but bids tend to come in late, and we were pleased with the arrangement and the final result was a win-win for both parties. Julie and Scott helped me enormously to set up the auction physically within the Baitson's showrooms. This gave prospective bidders the opportunity to view first hand all of the merchandise that was being auctioned off.

I was fortunate to be able to collect many Hull City Pre-War programmes, and at one point was the proud owner of 1930 FA Cup Semi Final

Hull City v Arsenal played at Aston Villa and also the replay at Leeds. I currently have a lot of my early Hull City programmes and ephemera on the Hull City 'Senior Tigers' website and to this day have several pre-war Hull City football programmes in my collection. I have, over the years, been able to obtain many programmes for my own collection and also spent hours swopping, selling and researching football programmes and memorabilia. An hilarious episode was meeting up with someone I didn't know or indeed recognise... but he was a very famous actor I was told. This happened at the Hilton hotel at Wembley, after the FA cup final of 2014, when Hull City almost beat Arsenal. It was after the game at the hotel when this person approached me to ask if I had seen Ken Wagstaff (who was a former Hull City Player) I said I hadn't and we exchanged pleasantries about the game. After joining my family who were in fits of laughter, they said do you know who you have been talking to? I said, No I haven't a clue! They said it was the actor, Tom Courtney.

CHAPTER THREE
EARLY LIFE &
MUSICAL YEARS

We go back to 1963 when I became infatuated with The Shadows as a group and with the brilliant instrumentals. I dreamed of the day when I could emulate Hank Marvin. Alas, this was not to be, as although I learned the guitar as I have mentioned, I was never really fast enough in technique or confident enough to be able to replicate on the stage as a lead guitarist. I have though, I believe, always had a good ear for music though and enjoyed this from a very early age. I could pick out music on dad's wireless and also sounds that drifted into our garden from the nearby East Park on most summer weekends. Listening to Radio Luxembourg was an early baptism to this wonderful new innovation to me that I had encountered. Some local friends, Iain

Watkinson and John Cook, were playing skiffle and practising with their instruments when invited me in with my plastic ukulele (which I was only just beginning to understand how to tune up never mind play the thing). I progressed to learn some ditties and really longed for a guitar. I spent hours rehearsing small riffs and ideas in the front bedroom I was born in. I always knew that's where I wanted to be- with entertainment and music. It became a big part of what I wanted to do, and hopefully achieve, to the highest level I could reach. I followed the UK tours of new pop stars and attended locally based shows when I could afford to.

Back to my school days, as I had aforementioned, I was very fortunate to be chosen by our school to sing solo at the Christmas concert for Hull schools held each year at the Hull City Hall. I sang to the dulcet sounds of 'Gloria in Excelsis' as an eleven-year-old. I still to this day recall quite vividly that experience. The Hull City Hall, although now quite outdated in many ways, still holds a special place in my memory as fantastic music venue.

My Son, Gareth, also had the distinction of playing violin in the local Schools' orchestra, in this prestigious building, on a number of occasions.

'I DON'T LIKE CRICKET! I LOVE IT!'

As a very keen sportsman although, I loved football, I did turn very much also towards cricket. Our schoolhouse team managed some great victories, and my best ever bowling feat of 7 wickets for 1 run still stands, I understand, today. This was at Primary school level.

In the seniors our Headmaster was Mr R.W Dallas, who was a lovely person, and he adored cricket. It was under Mr. Dallas I learned good batting techniques. I was chosen by my senior school Alderman, Cogan High, to represent an East Hull side against West Hull which served as a trial for Hull schoolboys representative side. I managed 22 runs in that game with the famed Ainthorpe High schoolteacher, Fred Ramsden, in charge of proceedings. Unbeknown to many, I played two matches against Sheffield at Reckitts Recreation ground in Hull and an away fixture at Doncaster. Another schoolfriend, Gordon

Suddaby, also played at this level and he was an outstanding batsman and became a good friend to me also. Gordon, as mentioned in this book, also played bass guitar for a short while in the Semi-Tones. I think we were all a bit gutted he was leaving to join up with the RAF. I do think my friend David Bell had some influence, although, looking back it served both of them very well, with Gordon completing a very long period of service and David who managed a 9-year stint himself.

Mr Dallas (the Head) was a massive cricket follower too and took a few of us under his wing and our school team and also at under 15 level our school team was very successful and we won our East league. In the shield final we were beaten by Westbourne High (winners of the West league) I still have the medal and certificate in my possession, to look back on from time to time. My best days at school, looking back, were the sporting days without any doubt. RWD became a Vicar in his latter years at Howden Church near Goole. What a marvellous character he was and admired by most pupils. In later years, well 14-16 years of age, I played competitive league cricket for firstly Reckitt's AN XI and to this day an unbeaten opening stand when we set up a first wicket partnership against Hodgson's of Beverley. With 136 runs for the first wicket. My opening partner, John Gray, made 68 runs. I managed 69 runs, and at the tender age of only 16 years of age, we won the match convincingly! I furthered my cricketing career by being selected for the first team and had wonderful occasions with being on the field with such great cricketers as: Les Turner, (what he could do with the seam on his bowling was nobody's business)   super-fast Peter Bacon, (another great cricketing fast bowler and smashing fella) John Saville, (a boycott style stubborn opener,) and Colin Hockney (who was by far the best wicket keeper I have ever played with). Dad, mum, and my brother Howard came down regularly to watch on the revered 'Recreation Ground'.

Reckitt's cricket team, between 1969 and 1973 won the Amateur League Division 1 on all of these consecutive years. It is now a league long gone, as too is the wonderful Recreation ground, completely sold off for building to profiteer. In playing myself, I often think of if I had continued to play at that level, would I have advanced much further? But then again as an entertainer I could not afford the time for cricket. So, it was take your pick, one or the other, and a tad like golf, cricket takes up a lot of time. A match can commence at 2pm and finish as late as 8pm, that's 6 hours, which can be a long day.

Alas, as I have mentioned, due to my growing work in live entertainment, I basically stopped cricket until the early 1990's, when I played locally in Hull for East Park CC. I had some good moments with them and playing with my brother Howard gave me a lot of satisfaction too. Our dad always came to watch our home games at Malet Lambert High School.

An amusing incident happened because Howard always took his two boys to cricket. One particular time we were playing away at Hutton Cranswick on the village green. The game suddenly came to a complete halt when his youngest son, Matthew, fell into the duck pond.

Everyone was rushing to stop him from drowning. Hilarious in the end, but by god it was water that stopped play rather than rain which is the usual cause! And yes, he was ok, but just soaking wet through!! My brother Howard was an excellent cricketer, much better than me, he achieved a massive milestone in his cricketing career managing 127 Not Out against BR North in 1990. A former school colleague John Hamson (never at his most friendliest) was hammered all over the ground by Howard. I scored 18 and have a presentation illustrated plaque to commemorate, as I was hit bodily everywhere you can think of, and an end of season presentation to me with a framed illustration showing this in caricature form.

Dave Orriss v. B.R. North - Season 1990

As a 19-year-old I signed for Pelican AFC in the Hull Sunday football league and did we have a great team! Tex Milne, who was the 'King' of country music in our area, hosting a regular Sunday slot on Radio Humberside also managed our football team at the Pelican Hostelry. We won the Hull Sunday league Division 7 in our first season and during the second season we won The Mary Halford Cup.

Such great players like Billy Teall (his dad was a Hull FC player in his time), Les Turner, (Yes, the star cricketer mentioned in the book) Alec

Campbell, Mally Wright great centre Back, myself at Left back, Vic Saville top player at right back (whose son eventually went on to play regularly for Hull City none other than Andy Saville who went on to make over 100 appearances for his home town club). I have met Andy on several occasions on my duties at the stadium, swopping stories too. We also had the joker of the pack Dave Smith in goal. What a character was Dave. Most matches, because we controlled the park, Dave had little or nothing to do. He would have a cigarette or be talking to someone behind the goal. Dave has run a very successful carpet fitting business over the years and to this day still has a shop on Holderness Road, Hull. Dave did brilliant though, as he suffered from Polio as a youngster, and for me he is a really top man!

The only let down, which saw the demise of that club, was whoever was the treasurer. All the cash went missing and no one ever knew what happened to it.

I had some great friends at school amongst them, Graham Roberts, David Bell, Stuart Sorrie, and Geoff Johnson amongst many others. in mentioning Geoff Johnson... He came to me at the summer school fair and said he was running a raffle and had 'borrowed' his mum's handbag as a prize. He said, "If I give you this ticket, I will draw it out and I can give you the handbag, and later on you can give me back the handbag, as my mother will kill me if I don't go back home with it."

The issue was, as a cricketer, I was batting on the field for the school Vs staff game, and I had obviously overstayed my welcome at the crease in which the draw for the Geoff's handbag had been made and he had to give his mum's handbag to someone else. Mayhem followed!

We supported Hull City and often went to watch matches both home and away. We spent many times together, usually football related. Both playing, watching, and playing Subbuteo table football games. Geoff Stubbs, a friend of Stuart, who was a Malet Lambert student had his Subbuteo set up in his front room in nearby Whitworth Street and I often used to look through the front window to see which teams he had on the pitch. These are still talked about today. Only recently at a football convention at **MKM** Stadium on 07/04/2022 I met an old friend and fine referee, Trevor Rose, who said he still remembers coming to our Lee Street home when we regularly hosted Subbuteo football competitions and leagues. The house was always full of kids. Mum and dad must have got fed up with all this, but as a child yourself you did not even think that way, did you? We also organised street teams for outside on the field matches, these were by and large set up by Geoff Stubbs and Stuart Sorrie. We had East Park Rangers, Reckitt United, Lee United, Rensburg Rangers, and others. We played a league and I fondly remember people like Stuart Sorrie, Derek Uzzell, and Colin Rollinson who ran their respective teams. We even printed a programme or two. Halcyon days, the summers lasted forever, the days were long, the sun shone through, and life was just a bowl of cherries. No mobile phones, no cans of drinks, no televisions, just a football, or ball and bat and life was just perfect really.

As pals we often went to away day football matches. One in particular stood out when we all went to see Sheffield Wednesday play Manchester United at Hillsborough. On the train we opened our lunches and Geoff Stubbs made us all howl with laughter. As he opens his pack up that his mother had prepared, he retorted 'Not enough here to feed a starving mouse!' Loads of laughter and how we enjoyed our away days!

When I was around 15 years old, our family booked two weeks at Hemsby near Great Yarmouth for a summer holiday. Lo and behold the Searchers, Gerry and the Pacemakers, and The Fourmost were all on the same bill at a Sunday concert at the ABC Theatre while we were there. We also went to the Great Yarmouth Windmill Theatre to see Joe Brown, the Tornados (massive hit with 'Telstar'), Rolf Harris, Peter Jay & The Jaywalkers. Well! seeing these convinced me that I should be up on the stage doing exactly the same myself. I was smitten for life! Managed to get a photo of Clem Cattini and some autographs, including the now infamous

Rolf Harris, who drew a picture of himself and wrote in my autograph book 'Little Pig, Busy Street, Motor Car, Sausage Meat' Never forgot that and never realised our paths would ever cross again... Which you will read it did in Malta!

At school I had always loved going on stage and totally making a fool of myself, which got laughs from the audience, but usually a scolding from the teaching staff! It was all about being the centre of attention looking back I believe. I once learned the lines as an understudy to a very comical lad at the school called David Chick. Now David had gone off ill three days before the concert was to take place, and I feverishly learned all the lines and even took part as a 'stand in' at the dress rehearsals. But my 'ego' came down many notches when David appeared on the afternoon of the concert, and I was so gutted at the young age I was. I see David occasionally as he lives not far from me from time to time and he is a fab lad just as I remember him then.

CHAPTER FOUR
MY FIRST GROUP DAYS

I had progressed in learning guitar techniques and forever practising my vocal abilities, but I really needed to expand with the help of other musicians, and it just happened that dad saw an advert in the local Hull Daily Mail advertising for a rhythm guitarist who could sing a bit. I duly replied and received a telephone call from Molly Chapman who was the Manager of the group THE SEMI- TONES. They were quite local to me, and I went down to audition and found that one of the band members, Pete Loft, had a Watkins Rapier red guitar. Well was it the guitar or was it, Pete? I was so excited. Molly's son Brian was the drummer, although he was only 13 years old, he was a very promising one at that. Pete was great on instrumentals, and I think between us we taught each other musical inclinations. Then came Carol Peake who was our female singer. Carol had a good rocky voice and then a friend of mine Gordon Suddaby, mentioned in earlier dialogue (a schoolfriend), asked if he could join and he would learn to play bass guitar. Gordon however, did stay for only under a year, as in talking with David Bell who recently had joined the RAF had also convinced Gordon to do the same.

Sadly Gordon died a few years back aged 70 and rather strangely on his birthday. His fulfilment on the stage had hardly started before it finished and he moved on and unfortunately, I never set eyes upon him ever again.

This newfound interest began in November 1963 and after many practise sessions Molly began to book us into local youth clubs and several hostelries. After Gordon had departed into the RAF, Mick Millington, a bass player (sadly another departed friend) joined the group. The Granby Hotel in Hessle, Drogos Den at Skipsea, many, many youth clubs and we managed to get prestigious bookings at the Hull

City Hall, copious gigs at the Beverley Regal Ballroom venue thanks to Molly's negotiating skills. It was at this prestigious venue where I was lucky enough, at an early age, to meet up with the soon to be/ very famous MICK RONSON who went on to play with David Bowie and the Spiders from Mars. Mick at the time played with the Crestas and it was here I first met up with bassist Tim Myers as well, another entrepreneur in the making and has proved so over his current lifetime. Every Friday 3 groups performed, with 2 groups each Saturday, and we played that venue countless times. A star Friday gig was while playing at the Regal Ballroom we had Unit 4 Plus 2 on the bill. A fab group with a great No 1 hit 'Concrete & Clay' and 'You've Never Been in Love Like This Before'. These guys were tidily suited and very accommodating, and I spent an hour or so before the show swopping stories and experiences with these very affable guys.

Me, Carol, Gordan, Brian and Pete

– The Semi Tones, 1963

Brian, Pete, Myself, Mick & Margaret
- The Semi Tones, 1965

Another good venue each Saturday was
Bridlington Spa Royal Hall when we supported
many top names of the time. The Nashville
Teens, Tom Jones and the Squires, a great group
The Animals, The Who (who smashed a guitar
up sending stuff everywhere), the list was endless.
Interestingly we signed one receipt in error
belonging to The Who, it stated £150 for the
night's payment back in 1964 not a lot now but a
large sum then. We received £20 which on
average was reasonable for an unknown group.
Back to Tom Jones, fab as he was, but many do
not realise he is not a very tall man around 5'8"

tops, different to what others may perceive. We did enter a Beat Group contest at the Hull Skyline Ballroom, although we reached the semi-Finals the overall winners where 'The Riverbeats' a very good local group. This gave us a good insight into standards and made us realise what was needed to up our potential.

I left the Semi Tones to follow a further experience, or so I thought, and joined up to form a duo in what proved to be an ill-fated move that didn't last long. Sometimes clashes of personalities happen and nobody is right and nobody is wrong. I never stood still for very long and moving on was so important, because after all, life is far too short to hang around wasting time on a move that didn't bring me progress.

During the summer of 1966 (What a great year for England's World Cup winning football team that was! I actually watched the final while on a break at Butlins Filey.) I also managed to win a free week's holiday for a stage performance in a duo and qualified for the regional final of 'THE PEOPLE' Talent contest, again held at Butlin's Filey holiday camp. I met some great likeminded entertainers including Billy Hygate (now a cruise director) and we bonded well together during that week. Another nice lad was Colin Johnson, who came from Sleights near Whitby, a very good organist amongst other finalists. I then heard on the 'grapevine' that a group The Fabians were on the lookout in the late 60's for a new guitarist with vocal harmony abilities. Bert Peterson was the group's manager who, years later, I came across at a Hull Hostelry one afternoon at the Four in Hand pub on Holderness High Road. We did have a brief chat but never ever saw him again. I had a really enjoyable 2 years with this group making great music with great people. Amongst them was Mike Peterson (Bert's Son) lead guitar/ vocals, Mike Wright the loveable 'crazy' drummer, Tim

Myers excellent on Bass, and Keith a strong tenor vocalist.

Keith, Me, Mike Peterson,
Front = Mike Wright, Tim Myers

Keith, Mike Peterson, Tim Myers,

Me and Mike Wright

We waded through Beach Boys/ Tremeloes/ Dave Dee Dozy/ Mick & Tich, and all good harmony song covers. We worked a fair bit on the RAF Camps, none more notable at RAF Scampton, in the Bowmans Mess with the chart-topping Equals of 'Baby Come Back' fame. I remember getting stuck on a sandbank on the paddle steamer in the middle of the River Humber whilst going to a gig at RAF Waddington. We made it, but only just, as we stayed stuck on a mud bank for 45 minutes. The Paddle steamer brought other memories. While with the Semi-Tones we took part in a few 'Riverboat Shuffles' on the River Humber, entertaining passengers who drank well and danced the evening away during those balmy summer nights!

THE MONTANA BROTHERS

It was at this stage shortly afterwards that I met up with the amazing **ALBERT BARLEY** who totally changed my life. Albert's Mum, Dora, was Italian and had met Albert's Dad, Fred, whilst serving during the war in Italy in WW2... and the rest as they say, is history. My mum and Albert's Mum eventually worked together as Usherettes at a local Hull cinema, The Cecil, through our friendship.

His brother Fred was also a competent vocalist and no mean slouch on the drums either and, like Albert, was a smashing fella to be with. Albert was in the 'Skysounds' group and was a very good lead guitarist in a very busy group. Complimented with Derek in the brass section, Lynda, a fab female singer, and managed by Phil Parkman Senior. It was his daughter Janet who eventually became Albert's wife.

The meet up happened as I applied for a position in the group as they needed another guitarist/vocalist. Nothing materialised as the transition of the Skysounds was happening. It was in conversations with Albert that we decided it would be good if we could work together. Although it was a month or so later before we actually did, which was mentioned in an earlier account.

So at this point Albert left the Skysounds. We had some really memorable gigs over the next few years and we often utilised the talents of both Phil Parkman Junior, and Albert's brother Fred who both played drums.

We travelled far and wide and I will always have a place in my heart for my lifelong best friend Albert. We gigged from 1969 to 1975 both semi-pro and professionally all over the UK, and had great times as mentioned throughout this book. Albert and I were really great bosom pals and our act became very slick, organised, and top notch.

We had many offers coming our way over the next few years in which we travelled many miles to ply our trade. As I mentioned, Albert and I developed a real bonding relationship as we were away from home so much, but very sadly, many years later he is no longer with us... passing in 2013. He was without doubt, the best and kindest pal I have ever had. I visit his resting place whenever I can and I have a lot of time too for his dear wife Janet, who is a very lovely person, and I keep in touch with his first daughter Joanne via social media.

Joanne lives in northern Italy on Lake Maggiore and speaks fluent Italian and is a very successful sales entrepreneur in Real Estate. We first met up through Tim Myers, who I had had contact through his days with Mick Ronson, as he phoned me and said he had met up with Albert Barley and thought it would be good to arrange a get together, with a view to forming a trio.

Now Tim was a lovely fella, and a great bass player at that, and we would arrange a rehearsal and he would stop for an hour or so then needed to be off. He had an array of friends in both male and female, and being a good looker he attracted the same in the female fraternity. Albert and I had visions of wanting to go pro and I had to break the news to Tim that was the way we wanted to go, so we parted company, and began our forage as the Montana brothers.

In the early days that Al and I were together, we often had time on our hands and having met up with Derry, an entertainment agent in Harrogate, he introduced us to wash leathers which was his main occupation. We have always, in the past, had an open type of market in Hull's old town. We knew Harry Harris, an accomplished pianist in his own right, he had the right contacts for us, and he had a costume jewellery stall in the market himself. He engraved most of his items he sold when people would visit him with their own purchases for engraving too. I did actually learn this off Harry, and to this day I can engrave reasonably well.

Harry was a real character, and he knew everyone. He introduced us to Johnny Firewood (love the name) who dealt in fabrics, and we were able to get our own shirts manufactured at a fraction of the cost you would pay in a retail shop. He had a few illicit goings on with a few girlfriends, but we really put that to one side without enquiring too much.

A spare stall was negotiated and so then taking a trip to Otley to meet up with Derry, who put us onto some super chamois leathers and off cuts, and we sold them at the market next door to

Harry's stall each Tuesday. Some great characters came to see us. Noel Talbot a great comedian of his time came and spent £5 on full chamois leathers. That was a lot of money in the early 1970's and he turned a lot of heads arriving in his Mercedes SL Sports car model. Another character of the time was Mark Conrad another variety artiste. He used to have us in stitches telling us that he had a keyboard but never ever played it. He used backing tracks to cover this up and no one ever cottoned on to this. He told us he said he was writing a book called 'Death of A Trawler' which in all honesty was not funny as it was the period when 3 local trawlers had vanished beneath the waves. This caused much distress and unhappiness to relatives and friends who had their loved ones on board these vessels.

We always were in awe of Mark as he had a much younger girlfriend than himself and could always pull when he needed to. He worked a regular gig at the Queens Hotel in Withernsea where he lived and booked artistes like ourselves for regular appearances. A true character and very comical at the best of times. Noel Talbot did a few seasons in Jersey at 'The Hawaiian' Portelet Bay which is where I next caught up with him. He then went to on to Australia working for many years. When we worked away we had the opportunity to do daytime activities. By staying at a B & B in the St. Helens area we often popped along to Wigan Baths which had an olympic sized pool where we spent time catching up on our swimming prowess. We often took in a football match when we could and took to the shops for a bit of retail therapy. If the occasion allowed, we would also learn new material and rehearse if we were able to.

Another amusing time when Albert and me worked together was often, if we were given a local gig by Don Holden, he would double us up for a late night job at Bridlington Club 61. We had to pack up quickly at the social venue and motor the 30 or so miles to the Promenade in Bridlington, up the stairs, no mean feat after already been working a full night performing, to be met with the white suited Tony Anfield the owner. Every time he would say 'thought you weren't coming' but 'I've held them for you'.

What he meant by that we were never quite sure. This venue never had many people in, but I know from clients in the venue he very much favoured our presence. Another situation worthy of a mention is that on the way one night to Club 61 we broke down. The kindest most lovely couple stopped and asked if we needed help. In short, we unpacked our gear, and they had a tow rope, which we attached to this couple's vehicle. They took us to the venue, we did the show, they supported us at the venue, took us to their flat where we stayed the night, then they arranged for a mechanic to sort our problem out. What a great gesture which we never forgot and did reward them with a gift and kept in touch for a long while afterwards. Someone up there does look after you! It is also so rewarding to be able to reward their kindness too.

CHAPTER FIVE
MUSICAL CHEERS!
ALBERT & ME!

It was the most wonderful period for entertainment, and being a part of the Montana Brothers duo in the early 1970's, we were looked after initially by Don Holden of McLeod/Holden Enterprises based in Hessle.

They really filled our diary, with Ian Gray also helping to overfill what we already had been given by Don, who periodically would call me and say, "Come into the office and bring your diary." Our first foray into the North-East through the agency where clubland was so very big, and on a good day the audiences were very receptive. This was a long weekend, with our first port of call at Houghton Le Spring WMC, our show was well received and after the show we travelled on to our B & B at Jimmy Butler's at

Roker View, Sunderland which was a pro artiste digs.

Over the years we continued to stay at Jimmy's, meeting up with many future top names such as, Nicky Stevens, a great vocalist who eventually joined "Brotherhood of Man'. Who would have thought that only a few years on from our Sunderland escapades, that Nicky would be a massive part of the group who actually won the Eurovision song contest with 'Save Your Kisses For Me' in 1976. Another rather amusing episode was that if you were a Hull 'born and bred' the Variety Artistes Federation (Localised only mind you, which really was a self-induced organisation that assumed leadership of all local artistes in that to work Hull venues) had you pass an audition to enable you to work.

This was not law of the UK, but simply a group of people taking over and telling local acts they must pass an audition in order to work. This though was a two edged sword, in that if you lived what was known as an 'Out Of Town act' you could be brought into work outside of this self-induced umbrella of being a localised act that had to prove your worth at an audition. Well, as a new act Al and I, as the Montana brothers, had to audition at the local Ambassador club and would you believe they failed us! The agents who had given us a full diary of work for the year could not understand why we should be turned down, although I knew it was a political move against our style of music. One said, "Well he is singing a song called Guantanamera in Spanish and that should not be allowed!"

"Bloody idiots out there," many artistes and club goers cried. A few phone calls and not so very long afterwards, this imitation organisation did disband!

Back to the North-East, and did we had some fun and frolics at Jimmy's. One night with everyone in on this prank, including myself, we had all being talking about how 'spooky' it was at Jimmy's place with things happening. Albert and I retired to bed and after about 20 minutes this strange looking female (Nicky Stevens, eventually part of 'Brotherhood of Man') opened the bedroom door, with lots of heavy green make up and a witches costume. He stepped in front of Albert by his bed and started making spooky echoing sounds into a microphone set up to a sound system, which looked and sounded very eerie! Albert leaped out of bed and the whole house was in uproar at Albert's reactions and frightened looks.

Albert was and still would be my very best friend I had ever had.

A similar occurrence happened when the 'Demon King' a wonderful person, who was appearing at the Sunderland Empire in the Christmas pantomime, caused mayhem when out of a bit of fun only, he leaped into bed with Albert. This saw Albert rush downstairs and outside. He would not come back in until we convinced him it was only a practical joke. There was so much frivolity after the shows, which always played a massive part of our lives in pro digs away from home.

Some years on we stayed at Norman Yule's Guest House down Tunstall Road, also in Sunderland. Now after a show all artistes are hungry. All energies spent on the stage usually resulted in massive hunger pangs. Norman always left 1 sandwich for each person in the act-only one! And a flask with some tea or coffee. Everyone returning from their shows were always starving, so we raided his fridge. We got a right rollicking and the next time we stayed there a lock had been fixed on the fridge to stop a re-occurrence by ravenous artistes. The problem was all 'take aways' in those days were literally closing at the same time as we were leaving the clubs, so eating was a no no as nowhere stayed open late anywhere. At Norman's we met up with many friends, some came only at weekends and some working full weeks. One such act Lenny Peters and Melody came up for long weekends of work in the clubs. Later on the world would know them as Peters and Lee. (Lenny and Diane). It made us laugh really as at the time, Lenny and Diane only came up for weekends and we were on 10 or 14 day runs. How tables turn, but good luck to them we would say as they were such lovely people. Another regular visitor was Dave Berry and the Cruisers and possibly the best mime business in the UK, The Discoes who were always in house when we visited the area. They were a complete unique mime act. Sadly, most of them are not with us now.

Towards the end of 1970 we were very fortunate (or so we thought) having negotiated by ourselves a 2-week season in Cardiff and the Valleys of South Wales for a really tough guy by the name of Don Tyrer. He was involved as a variety agent, and also looked after Joe Erskine a top boxer in his time, and his wife Betty ran a guest house within their home in Cardiff. Although Betty was a lovely lady, I remember one artiste was sat waiting, having been served at dinner (as we all had) a piece of cooked fish with a blob of potato on it. We all enquired why he wasn't eating it? He retorted that surely must be something else to add to the plate as surely was not enough to 'feed a starving insect!" Yes, the hospitality was way down the list and what with hunger pangs and her husband working us to death god knows how many shows per day, they must have been making a fortune out of all of us artistes each week. The first night of our 2 weeks dates and £200 net to us and no commission to pay! And this we boasted to everyone that we could tell as this surely is real money or so we thought. Our first gig we did in South Wales was at Watts Town WMC in the Valleys, the first night was on the Sunday and then back to Don's abode for a good night's sleep or so we hoped! We entered our room, a large front bedroom, but it had 7 beds in it. We were sharing with other acts (all male you see) but privacy... none! The next day Don Tyrer, the agen,t in a stern gruff voice said, 'Right you Montana Brothers it's Monday and you are at a Derby & Joan afternoon show in Barry. Tonight," he told us, "You are on to Cwmbran Working men's Club for one spot then on to Treforest WMC for another spot and finish up at Cardiff Gino's night club." 4 gigs in 1 day! God almighty! Altogether in 14 days we did 23 gigs with doubles and trebles etc, and we had a debate about the last night of the tour at a night club which was a double job, you did not pick money up, but they fed you with chicken in the basket. Do we starve and go straight back home or eat and live? We ate and did the show and fortunately lived! Always the sucker! Talk about exploitation!! Although the above relates in a somewhat, negative way, a lot of good came about due to a lovely comedian called Benny Britten from Sheffield.

Benny tipped us off about a certain Peter Groves PG Entertainments who was a well-respected cabaret agent in Cardiff. After calling him on the telephone he invited us into his office for an audition. We duly went and Albert slaughtered him with the 'William Tell Overture' on guitar, I played my bit with the guitar at the back of my head and contracts were immediately sought!

How Peter found them I do not know as his office was a complete tip, papers not just on his desk but all over the floor too, but find them he did.

We worked a lot of full week cabaret shows all over Wales and the South-West. Amongst others, we worked full weeks in cabaret at Exeter Riverside Club, Bristol Cadbury Court club, Bodmin Jail Nightclub, Perranporth Apollo Sands club, Dursley Raglan club, Leigh Garrick club, Falmouth club International club,

Webbington Country club, Usk Stardust club where we followed Cliff Richard. We worked well in cabaret with many, many others at the height of full week's working in top class clubs.

No doubting we had the cream of work, and only a stone's throw from making a breakthrough through our vast network of entertainment moguls and impresarios that saw both us contacting them, and the bookers viewing and checking up on us. Our first week for Peter Groves was at Cardiff Tito's Night club, without doubt the jewel in Peter's crown. A fabulous venue that as you entered an aroma which was a sweet smell of roses that never failed to impress and fire me up ready to do the show.

It was during January of 1971 that we were to appear with the great Ronnie Dukes and Ricky Lee and their band. Ronnie, of Jewish persuasion was very funny and came out with some comedy (which today would be too near the mark!) A particular one that I remember went like this, "Headline in the local press read - Arab dies with a thousand stab wounds... The

Jewish coroner said, it was the worst case of suicide he'd ever seen!"

Musically they were great too, with several of his family in the band, including the Mother-In-Law! And very talented on the piano, who took some banter from Ronnie. In watching others you learn so much, and Albert and I never missed one of the shows watching the techniques and how to use the stage to such an advantage.

We were halfway through our twice evening set on the first night when in walked Freddie and The Dreamers. I looked at Albert and he said, "Bloody hell I can't believe this!" They were appearing in pantomime at the Cardiff Sophia Gardens theatre. After our show and spending some time with them, they invited us to go to the next day's matinee performance and after seeing our performance at Tito's, we all went to a fabulous steak restaurant they had discovered. A pleasant night was enjoyed by us all.

Another appearance quickly followed at Tito's and on the bill was AL. T. Kossy, a comedian, and the hit parading trio The Settlers, a group with several hits to their name, including the

'Lightning Tree.' I always recall one of their quips on stage Mike, John and Cindy...

John said, "When Mike and I joined up, work was plentiful and 'we never had it so good', but when Cindy joined us 'we never had it so much'! Loads of great times and myrrh!

Another surprise for us both was a man introduced himself at the venue as 'Dick Ray' a major agent in Jersey of whom I was aware, but we had never met. He wanted us to accept an offer to work at 'The Watersplash entertainment venue' in St. Ouens Bay Jersey that same year. We did pencil this in for the following year however... But it was amazing to meet up with names we had read about and to actually have them approach you for work. Manna from heaven!

Jersey has for me had many wonderful moments both in entertainment and the sheer ambiance of this magical island. As I had mentioned, agent Dick Ray actually saw our act in Cardiff at Tito's club and offered us contracts on the spot. As a performer I worked at 'The Mediterranean' and also 'The Watersplash' both on St. Ouen's Bay at a time when a split in cabaret and the newer hotel seasonal approach to entertainment occurred. The summer season period usually lasted between May and September, with the smaller bars operating in the main July/August period when visitors reached their height of popularity each year. On each occasion I worked there it was essential to hire a vehicle for commuting although I was very lucky to meet and befriend a person by the name of Louis Le Grande who lent me a beat up automobile but save my putting in fuel, it cost me nothing except at the season end I always gave a free performance to thank Louis for his generosity and it goes without saying when he did me a favour and I returned it without any money changing hands. What an excellent idea being that money is the root of all evil?

I did meet some amazing individuals on the island and if it had been possible to purchase a dwelling I really would have. The only stumbling block is that in Jersey at the time I would have had to have £2 million in the bank to even qualify to even be allowed to bid for a property. I do believe matters are changing now somewhat but even so you would need masses of collateral to qualify for residency. The next best thing is to visit the island of which I must have taken in excess of 40 return flights over the years in business and in pleasure. Other islands within the Channel Islands part from Jersey include Alderney, Guernsey, Sark, Herm, Jethou, Brechou, Brecqhou and not all are inhabited. For instance, Jethou has 3 residents. The smaller Islets do not have residents.

It should be noted that two of my very good friends, Graham and Pat Roberts both worked on Jersey for a five-year period, not long after leaving school - and consequently there knowledge of the island and networking of people they knew assisted me in being able to secure not only friends but a lot of work at that time.

I cast you all back to Benny Britten the comic we met in South Wales. All of us acts had Tuesday free that week so he invited us all up to Barry Island to see his show. Now to us Benny was very, very, funny but being from South Yorkshire and having a South Wales audiences is not a good mix. Plus he began cracking jokes about Don Tyrer the agent, and his guest house ran by his wife Betty. We were in stitches but after his first set the club paid him off. Sadly, he was paid off most nights and his week was curtailed. A lovely guy that really deserved better respect though. He just went off the rails and played to us dozen or so that had gone along to see his act from the digs, taking the 'Mickey' out of Don and his wife Betty. Of course, the audience had not a clue what he was on about apart from our gang from the digs who were totally in stitches!

Another quip that I remember played a part of my cabaret act that went down well and always got a laugh was...

I have a safe at home and I always told my wife not to look in it, I went to the market last week and my wife looked in the safe.

I said, "I always told you not to look in the safe, and you have."

She said, "I found forty thousand pounds and three eggs in it."

She said, "Why have you got three eggs from our chickens in the safe?"

I said, "Well every time I have a relationship with someone else's wife, I put an egg in the safe."

The wife said, "Well I suppose that's not bad over 35 years."

I said, "No, you've got it all wrong... When I get a dozen eggs, I go to the market and sell them!"

We continued with our cabaret circuit by playing The Ocean Club also in Cardiff ran by two Mafia type men. Our treatment was not of the best that we could expect due to various matters such as band call times and re timings, complimentary drinks that never happened etc. One of the mobster types came and said we want you to go into the Valleys after your set each night here to play at Ocean Club 2. We will pay you fuel money. After what had gone on, we refused and lo and behold when we finished our week our Cheque 'bounced'! As we were back in Cardiff a month later, we managed to get our wages but that really struck a 'bum note' with us!

Next up was Bristol 'Talk of the West'. Rehearsal Sunday afternoon then playing through until the following Saturday evening. 1

show per night. Our 'Digs' based in Clifton was run as a show biz guest house. We met up with Maynard Williams (son of Bill Maynard) and other fine acts. It was there I met up with my first wife to be. After the last show on the Saturday night our overall 'management' had placed us at Willington WMC for a lunchtime show on the Sunday, meaning our 'management' had totally messed up, as we literally finished at 1am and then had to travel immediately through the night in our Morris Thousand van from the South-West to the North-East, too many miles for a lunchtime show. We arrived at Willington WMC Co Durham to be told we were not on there - great we thought! The committee man suggested did we mean Willington WMC Newcastle? So off we went. With 5 minutes to spare the 'committees' posse' were in the car park giving us a right telling off for being late-we didn't bother to explain ourselves and eventually arrived at the Sunderland digs. After the show where we both fell asleep on the carpet and was woken telling us we would be late for our evening show if we didn't get a move on. All in all, a very stressful couple of days. Without doubt some of the travelling to and fro was ridiculous, but other times it did work for us.

Back to our Bristol gig. We had replied to an advert in 'The Stage' for a summer season gig at the Sunshine Holiday Centre, Hayling island, on the south coast. It was the Tuesday and as we had the day off, we trundled in the 'Moggy Thousand van' all the way along the south coast to that very Holiday Centre for an invited audition. After arriving we were met by Ken Newington the General Manager and his son Peter who although was not an entertainer, but by virtue of nepotism, he had become the entertainments manager by proxy. They liked us however, and we were given a 24-week season commencing rehearsals in the March.

While we were in rehearsals, we were mini bussed to a sports shop for a creme pair of trousers, this was to complement our Maroon blazers with the holiday centre badge sewed on. We would wear yellow polo neck jerseys during the day but swopped for white shirts and a tie for evenings, except for our shows when we wore our stage costumes. It should be noted that we followed two names that have become very synonymous aka 'Chuckle Brothers' then known as the Harman Brothers. A couple of years earlier Rick Parfitt (of Status Quo fame) had the honour as lead act, so to follow those into the Sunshine Holiday centre was no mean feat! Well £50 a week between the 2 of us, of which if you stepped out of line in any way you had a financial deduction to contend with on top.

The staff who were really great to get on with consisted in order of appearance :- The Montana brothers (ourselves), Mary Steadman, vocalist with Dancers Jacqui Pym, Greg, Phil, Lynn Taylor vocalist, Yuleo, Weavers Green, Andy the Sports organiser. We put together several shows each week. We also had daytime activities which actually gave way to us earning a few extra bob!

During the daytime Phil asked to swop with me on the Car Racing Simulator as he found it tedious and boring. Although we were offered an end of season bonus it was never going to happen due to harsh financial penalties as aforementioned. So, after a word I swopped roles with Phil who wanted more daytime dance rehearsals. This simulator was popular with the punters. We had to take the money and issue them with a ticket. But I soon realised that if I held back two tickets out of four, it was possible to put 30p into our own pockets and over the session became a good little money earner during the daytime activities. On my day off Albert took my place. It was essential to keep this one 'in-house' as-to-speak. This trick was never rumbled and helped mitigate our losses due to fines for allegedly acting out of line with the management, or so they indicated. It wasn't that we did not get along, artistes and management stuck rigid to the house rules so in return we did our best to 'claw' some monies back as described.

The Donkey Derby was another good way to earn 'illicit' money too, until unfortunately after 3 months of success we were then found out! How this worked was each week the same donkeys would arrive for the races. We soon cottoned onto which was the fastest and by having a 'quiet' word with the rider and just tell him/her to hang on they would win and so would we! So, a bet was installed by a punter on our behalf, and we cut them in on the winnings. Highly immoral but a necessary deed to put into practise to enhance our increasingly decreasing cash we had in our bonus bank accounts due to the harsh financial penalties being imposed.

The season was going well, we had a 'cheerio' then a 'meet and greet' to do each Saturday morning when a change of guests occurred. Also and we all hated this, we had taking it in turns through the week as in turn the whole entertainment cast had to get up for an early morning spiel for Happy Birthdays and Anniversaries and singing first thing in the morning which is not recommended believe me! Each evening we were given a voucher for a cup of Horlicks to help us sleep well until the next day. Normally if not required on Happy birthday duties we managed a 9am get out of bed call as opposed to 7.30am for spiel time. A lot of the scripts in Hi-Di-Hi were carbon copies of our holiday centre involvements and indeed some of their film shots were taken at Sunshine Holiday

Centre where we resided, including The Film 'Confessions of A Holiday Camp' were almost all scenes were totally filmed there.

We had a camp football team and always had a good game and a laugh with our Guests v Staff matches. It's funny how both the staff and guests really took this very seriously as a lot of pride was at stake! Nothing was at stake really, except jolly banter we could have through the week with the guests. Evenings belonged to all the entertainers. We had club nights, cabaret in the theatre. We had evenings devoted to our own shows with harmony vocals dancing and the like with our team. We always had lots of fun. We also had a visiting male artiste named Yuleo. Now Yuleo was a definite one off. He was as bald as a coot but had this conspicuous wig which kept moving from one side to another. It never actually fell off, but one of the entertainment team played a trick on him. On one of his songs a Tom Jones favourite he would reach for the high note and failed miserably as he could not reach it. At that pointing the dancers performing behind Yuleo came into an embrace momentarily with him but instead of moving on one female dancer quickly dislodged his wig and he was left with him still singing and his wig hit the deck! Everyone was in stitches and much of the audience who thought it was part of the act. From then onwards Yuleo's wig never took further part in the show! What a spoilsport!

We did however, have an evening when the theatre became a cinema and that gave us all a night's rest which most of us spent chilling or sleeping. Our homes were in the upstairs of the 'Welcome Inn' where our joint shows took place but downstairs of course! It was very quiet as the cinema took place in the theatre, so it was a quiet evening for all above in our small rooms. So apart from our usual nightcap it was the entertainments' staff night off! I was on the rota, put down to do a running commentary, early evening one night a week on a model battleship fight on the large pond. It never went right as most ships sunk after they had been launched. The system was flawed from day one and the manager gave it up as a bad job and immediately deducted a further minus from my end of season bonus. I used to say to Albert "If I am minus nothing what happens?" He used to say "don't even go there!"

CHAPTER SIX
HOMEWARD BOUND

Our season however sadly ended abruptly, when Albert announced that due to his girlfriend becoming pregnant in the middle of the contract, the season would have to be curtailed and we were to return back home. So basically, if Albert left so did I as we were a team and almost joined at the hip anyway! We did a bit of a moonlight flit but needs must! The management had not helped in many ways, so it worked out it was the best for all concerned.

After travelling home, my dear dad, who was always there to help us in any way he could, managed to find me a job back at Reckitt and Colman in Hull. Albert could have had a job also but elected to go back into carpet sales, so he politely refused dad's offer. I did however, work from the bottom so as to speak, and dad managed to arrange an interview with the service gang Foreman Wally Garfitt. Wally, I found, was a very genial guy and I accepted the different room service jobs he asked me to do. Such as looking after production lines, moving pallets with an electronic bogie, and eventually moving into Lem-Sip, (At that time under Harry Braimbridge another super foreman who was a great pal of my dad) an up-and-coming pharmaceutical product to help colds and the like, which is now a household name course.

I did meet several good people whilst working as a labourer, including Ken Wilkinson who without doubt became my best mate. We shared laughs and sporting likes and spent a fair bit of time within each other's company. (Sadly, I have to add at this point I have just found out that he has recently passed, and although I hadn't seen Ken for many years, I valued him as a very good friend. With wonderful memories almost working together but in the same area, so we always came across each other. He always said he thought he would like to be a lift attendant but had second thoughts as he thought 'it might be too many ups and downs as an occupation!) Along with Ken's brother Alan who was just as genial as Ken. We played in the summer 5 a side football team on the Reckitt's recreation ground during those early 70's and had some really special social moments.

Musically, we did however, continue on a semi-professional basis for another 4 years or so which turned out well. As a duo The Montana Brothers worked with some big names before anyone was aware of them. For instance, Paul Daniels when we did a full week in Hull venues, and he cut my head off at Piper club and Golden Key clubs (I must have survived the first one to take the next one I suppose). Also we crossed paths with Lynne Perrie and Liz Dawn a couple of times of Coronation Street fame and a Cameo role with Roy Barraclough(Alec Gilroy). Which I will enlarge on later.

Having met my first wife Gill down in Bristol earlier in 1971 whilst working at the 'Talk of The West' night club and mainly down to the logistics we decided to tie the knot on 28 August that year.

The number 28 has played a most significant part of my life, in that it was the day I married on 28 August 1971 at St. Martins Church, Knowle, Bristol. My second wife Julie was born on 28th April, my youngest Son Scott was born on 28th June and exactly the same day (28th) as Hull City AFC was formed in 1904 and equally the same date that Henry VIII was born (none other than) and various friends of ours, including my Sister-In-Law Sue's on 28 February all have that same day as their birth days too. Our house number as a child was 218 Lee Street so the number 2 and 8 came about in that house number too. We lived at 28a Hull Road, Cottingham for a few years during the early eighties. And mum and dad's friends Frank and Betty Smith, with Christine and Keith their children, lived at 28 Walgrave Street in Hull.

Interestingly but in a different way, both Julie's and my parents. by coincidence, married on 16 March in their respective years. So we decided in 1991, as 16th March fell on a Saturday, it would be most appropriate to choose that day for our register office wedding too. It made sense as no one in either family could forget the date of our very same wedding anniversaries. We had a fabulous reception that Saturday afternoon in Pearson's club, in Hull and we made our own entertainment as 'Driving East' with Glenn, Hughie, and Julie and I on tambourine, entertaining our guests at the wedding breakfast. We had all our guests at Both the ceremony and the reception which we both thoroughly enjoyed. We then took the train for a few days in London on honeymoon.

However, my first marriage, although lasting some 17 years, was never going to finish in harmony. It goes without saying that life for me was work, life for her was bringing up the kids and yes, I do have regrets with not being around at times. However, despite all this we built a sound home. At the back end of the relationship 1983-86 we lived in a house with one and a half acres of land, but looking back to what end did that assist any of us? Our daughter was 16 and Son was only 10 when we split. In those days in the courts the man was normally accepted as the 'bad guy' and that reverberated in settlements too.

I did not bother to go for custody as my lawyer said it would be a waste of a day and it would never happen, so I took his projected advice. Sadly, because of the split I have not had the time with either my son or daughter that I had wished for, however, I am hopeful for the future.

CHAPTER SEVEN

MOVING UP AT RECKITT'S!

My first forage into working at Reckitt's came about by my dad in 1963, when he rescued me from RD McLeish, the Bakers, based in Hull and Cottingham. I had moved into working as an Apprentice Baker following a wasted 6 months or so as a 'runner' for a local fishing and fish manure company. Working in the bakery had good memories for the most, except that the work was quite full on in a physical way, but the company of my work colleagues overrode the working side. The main contentious issue was at the age of 16 I was asked to start work at 6am. Well at that time it was really not good for a 16-year-old on a pittance of a wage to commence work so early. Yes, it was an earlier in the day finish, but for a growing lad it was not conducive to good socialising the previous evening and not at all helpful to the pocket monetary wise.

Another highlight was taking Sheila on my first ever date. Sheila was a girl I had noticed as I often took bread into the shop from the bakery, which was at the rear of the building. What made the date so memorable was that I had bought 2 tickets to see the Rolling Stones at Hull City Hall and finally plucked up the courage to ask her out. The show was at a time when the Stones had their first record 'Come On' in the charts and amongst others on the show were Johnny Kidd & The Pirates, Heinz and the Wild Ones, Sammy King & The Voltaire's. (In later years I worked with Sammy whilst in the same management i.e. Flair Theatrical Agency) Local group The Aces with Eric Lee, Johnny Paterson and co. A standout date but I never plucked the courage to ask Sheila out again, so it was not meant to be. Because of my interest in sport and music, I never really indulged in the female fraternity properly until I was around 20 years.

Yes, my dad eventually had a word with the overall boss at the bakery, Bob McLeish senior, and as a result I left and lo and behold I was given an interview at Reckitt's Ltd for a general labourers' vacancy that had just occurred. I must have held a decent interview (or a bit of nepotism) so I was given the job working in the Old Mill, on the Stoneferry site, as a Serviceman at the interview.

This work involved keeping machines working by changing bins as lids and bottom were manufactured on piece work by the young lady operational teams. This was a noisy, massive, room with productivity at its highest. The Foreman in the room was affectionately known as 'Wacker' and everyone was pretty much scared of him excepting for Dorothy Philips who was the forewoman of that room.

Whilst working at this new position my dad, who arguably pulled some big sway at this company, interviewed through Personnel a certain Arthur Bunting who was setting the rugby league world on fire with scintillating performances on the rugby field with Hull Kingston Rovers. Now Arthur was someone I just loved as a person.

Often on a Monday morning, after a weekend game, he could barely walk so without anyone knowing, (the back room had a lot of bins with metal tops/bottoms but some containers were empty) Arthur soon found to his advantage that if you climbed up the steps, opened the top, climbed in and replace the top, that a good hour or two's sleep was what the doctor ordered.

People were forever trying to locate him, but only I knew where he was. Nowt to do with me, I kept schtum but for months nothing changed. Arthur was so likeable the bosses would probably have let him get on with what he wasn't doing if they had known!

Another guy I worked well with was Alan Pye. Now Alan sadly passed at a very young age, but he was one of the most transparent persons I have been privileged to have known. He loved my rendition of the song 'Long Tall Texan' he continually talked about this whenever we were working together.

Harold Bruce, a great friend of my dad, worked in the same room too. Harold was just one nice fella to know, even years later I bumped into him in the town centre, it was always a pleasure to have time with this very likeable co-worker. It was a pleasant time but as always, I was keeping a look out on the notice board and one day I saw an internal advert for a pastry chef wanted at the Company's Dansom Lane site. So I applied, was interviewed by both Alan Scarr, the Manager, and Arthur Clinton, the head baker. Little did I know that my relationship with Arthur blossomed so much over the years and our paths crossed in so many ways. For instance, Arthur was a baker so was I, Arthur was a musician, so was I, I was doing TV Walk on Extra work in my spare time, I was able to get Arthur fixed up doing the same and to his credit he was in a short space of time working 2/3 days a week on Emmerdale Farm as it was known then.

Reckitt's Bakery, Arthur Clinton & Me

We did so much together, and although his family life was not what it should have been, for me I have always liked the work ethic that Arthur showed me. He would always say 'No True Artist Ever Calls His Work Hard' That has always stayed with me, but for all his ways it did not always go down with his working colleagues in the canteen where we worked. In later life he worked for me in one of the newsagents that we ran. Yes, I loved Arthur as a dear friend and confidant.

I attended his funeral many years later and sadly only 3 of us and his dear wife Edie minus his two sons turned up at the Crematorium. I had much respect even though he could be a hard taskmaster, his work ethic helped me so much to be the person I am today. I do miss you dear friend.

My philosophy has always been to take tasks on whether it be work or otherwise, see it through and look for even greater opportunities. After all, we all have one go at life, why not make the most of every possibility.

It was a wrench in many ways, as I have mentioned previously, to leave a work place that I enjoyed but I always found myself looking over my shoulder for more fruitful and exciting opportunities. I always remember too that

Arthur Clinton always said, "You will have to work for the rest of your life." But I always thought inwardly, 'yes, but on my terms and not others that might 'pigeon hole' you for the rest of your working days.' I have always carried a very strong 'work ethic' and am at my happiest really when in this environment. Yes, I love my family but as the only bread winner of substance, I have the in-built need to do this. To keep everyone in a stable way in life's long path.

Back in the halcyon days of the early 1970's I managed my way from the shop floor at Reckitt's to the dizzy heights of full time Secretary of the ASTMS Union within the company over a two-year period. All whilst still maintaining my active entertaining roles. Now the ASTMS was Association of Scientific and Technical Managerial Staffs (sorry I swallowed a dictionary) was the main white collar union for this multi-national company I worked for.

ASTMS Representatives
(From Left: Ron Dawes, Roy Farnill, Jim Tiplady, Me, Front:
Dick Walker)

We had some amazing success over a pay dispute at one point. The company were getting more and more vexed with our continuous assault on their financial holdings, when our regional manager Dick Walker, a great Scotsman (you can always tell a Scotsman, but you can't tell him much!) Spotted in one of the back and forth of written offers suggestions and the like, one particular paragraph that said I.e. we will offer you a 3.4% rise. Now, Mr Walker being very astute and said 'hang on did they mean e.g.' (which means 'for example' as we all know) but he said 'I.e.' which is Latin for THAT IS! A whole different meaning. We brought this to the Personnel Director leading the company's discussions. He refused to accept what I.e. meant - 'That Is' so please pay us a 3.4% raise in our wages. He flatly refused, so Dick, on the union's behalf, registered a 'failure to agree' on the wage negotiations. We registered this with ACAS which is 'Advisory, Conciliation and Arbitration Service' at City House in Leeds, and together with the management we all took the train to Leeds.

Now City House is part of the Leeds railway station buildings so only a few hundred yards walk and we had arrived! We went through all details with the tribunal and lo and behold they gave us the thumbs up! We had won this argument and it cost the company a significant amount of cash. The next day we held a meeting for members and gave them the news. They were ecstatic and we were all given a standing ovation on the success of our challenge by the membership the very next day. Sadly, the Personnel Director was never seen again, last leaving for Norwich to ply his trade at the Colman's subsidiary. All in all an amazing time of which I then went on to work for the 'other side' as a Personnel/Welfare Officer within the company for a period prior to my business dealings. I always felt my mentor was another Personnel Manager by the name of Pat Haynes. Pat was a very inspiring lady who encouraged me to pursue my next move in employment. We worked well together as a Union to Management team and I had so much respect for such a really lovely person.

I had at that time an opportunity to leave the Hull area but still working for the same company and this would have meant moving lock, stock, and barrel to another area. I pursued the opportunity of expanding my ambition of business interests instead.

CHAPTER EIGHT
INTO BUSINESS

I have omitted that whilst working in Personnel or 'HR' as it has been known in USA and now known as this here as well today, (Yes, we are usually 10 years or so behind America) I proceeded to purchase my first ever retail business. It was in a very small low roofed abode, but on a busy main road leading out of the city. We purchased a newsagent's business for the princely sum of £8,000 and the people we bought off were nearing retirement so it seemed a perfect opportunity to start up. On the first day my first customer bought a small packet of Golden Virginia tobacco, never forgot that. I had opened up at the unearthly hour of 4.30am as trade picked up quickly from that point onwards. My dad relieved me at 8am so I could go on to my normal working daytime duties within Reckitt's. This continued for a few months and although a transfer of work became a possibility from one city to another, my marriage was not good, so I had the opportunity of redundancy which I gladly took as a great opportunity to purchase another business which had surfaced.

It was indeed Wold Road newsagents. A very busy outlet in a large housing area. I had only been in situ for around 6 months when a fast-developing newsagent entrepreneur came in by the name of John Turnbull. Now John already had accumulated around 10 retail outlets and asked if I would be willing to sell to him? I mentioned that I had only recently purchased the business and was hoping to sort things out moving forward. Well John, if nothing, is very persistent and came in with an offer to buy the business. It was a few thousand short of double what I had paid for the outlet. I said I will give it some thought. By countering the bid I suggested if he upped the payment by a few more thousand and it was a done deal. He accepted on the spot. So, my foray into retail outlets had begun in earnest.

A point about accountants. There are accountants that work for their clients and ones that work hand in glove with the authorities. No doubt about that! Enough said, we had Mark that worked with the latter. He took me to court for an amount he knew I could not pay at that time and then had the audacity not to bother to turn up for a hearing (as he thought I would not turn up myself, wrong!) He was later paid cash in full that which was owed to him. No friend of mine and hope our paths never cross in any way again. He was just a ruthless freak to me and never anywhere near a friend.

In later life though, my next and last accountant of many years was Paul Whiteley, he did a wonderful job in that we as a small business had previously got lodged with a chartered accountant who knew no bounds on the prices he charged us. Paul retrieved a four-figure sum for us. Paul for the small business as we had, did a fab job in the mid-nineties and what a lovely person he is to deal with. At one point our first family was the proud owner of 4 outlets, three in Beverley Road and one in King Edward Street, all in Hull. It was a mammoth task and apart from helping with the Vat and books, my wife at the time, spent more time with others and spent less and less time within the outlets. No one knew of her whereabouts, so it was always going to be difficult to carry on, as work was not compatible between us and a split was inevitable. I too was not blameless, in fact far from it, but our different movements in life caused the split at a time when my daughter was 16 and first son was 10. not ideal.

However, its water under the bridge and I have no wish, for lots of valid reasons, to ever look back as I have great understanding and compatibility with Julie who has been my current partner and wife for 33 years. We have two wonderful sons that have been a pleasure to see growing up and developing themselves. They have become a total credit to us both. But backtrack, some, 10 years plus!

We were fortunate to have news boys who played at a high level by entering a team at the local news federation competition – we only went and won it! We had however, two members of this team that played for Hull school boys – who were outstanding players.

Photograph taken prior to the final at
Wembley Stadium.

We then went onto the regional finals, and dare I say, we won that too! A competition that was played in Bradford. This then took us on to the Grand National Finals – that was held at

Wembley – the news federation organised a coach to take the team and supporters down to London for the big day, during the competition finals we won and got through to the grand final so it was D & G News V Mini Marines of Kent as half time we lead 2-0 but alas we tired, and we were pipped at the final whistle losing 2-3 – but what an amazing achievement. All the lads received racing cycles as runners up and we were entertained by Councillor Woodford and his wife for a teatime experience at the Hull Guildhall.

CHAPTER NINE
NEW HORIZONS

Musically by 1975, we decided as an act to part, always on good terms in that an overseas deal had been secured and Albert with his new arrival needed time at home understandably. In that time, I had some excellent work as a solo entertainer coming in, and the three summers of 1975, 1976, and 1977 working for 'Thomson's Holidays Rest of the World department' for Eric Galloway management, in London, and working the international entertainment circuit throughout the summer months.

I appeared in Malta Sliema Preluna Sky room night club on 3 occasions, Malta Mellieha Pagoda room Hotel, Corfu Roda Beach hotel, Portugal Lisbon Estoril La Guincho Hotel, Rimini Hosteria del Castello Nite club, Tunisia Sahara Beach hotels, Dubai Chicago Beach

Hotel and in Mallorca at Cala Bona Hotel Cala Bona.

Tommy Bruce and his wife Sheila were on the bill in Sousse, Tunisia and we became firm friends, visiting them in a village near Warrington in later years with my brother Howard. I took my first family with me on several of the trips to Portugal, Corfu, Malta and Tunisia. In Malta I worked with a very funny comedian Peter Wallis. We were on the same bill together at the Preluna hotel in Sliema. Funny man, funny jokes. "How do you make your own anti-freeze? Shove her knickers in the fridge." Peter was known as Peter 'Machine Gun' Wallis because of his incredible fast delivery of 'one-liners'.

I made a return visit the following year and worked with an act named Robin Good. Now Robin is a fine artist but the choice of us working together might have been looked at more closely as we both delivered a very similar act. We had mainly Cosmos and Thomson guests with one night a week devoted to the local Maltese. All this took place on the top floor in the Sky Room Nite Club at the Preluna Hotel in Sliema.

It was in Malta that I met up again from years back none other than Rolf Harris. Rolf was the owner of the Busket Roadhouse night club situated near M'dina, the silent city. A place I visited from time to time of which entertained with visiting guest artistes and a resident band.

In Corfu I nearly drowned! Well apart from a great venue at the Roda Beach Hotel and just across the bay was Albania which at that time was a really dark place to be. Albania was a communist regime with not much contact with the outside world. However back to the near fatality! The hotel was as described next to the beach. I decided in my wisdom to literally run into the water from the beach. In doing so at top running speed from the beach I literally plunged unknowingly to at least 10-15 feet below the surface in which I swallowed what seem noodles of salt water. I was struggling for breath when I surfaced and went under again as I came up for the second time a young Corfu resident got hold of me and dragged me back onto the beach and I was immediately quite sick and took a while to recover. Never went back into the sea ever again anywhere!

The show at the hotel went brilliantly with a great ovation and complimentary drinks by the management and apart from that incident, the trip was a roaring success. Lovely island which I would like to visit again someday.

Albert and me we always kept in touch over the years that followed, and indeed spent 1984-86 back as a duo again. After that point Albert decided he wanted to work solo as I had done and I thoroughly respected his decision. But sadly many years later in 2013 Albert passed after having difficult times fighting a debilitating illness. I can honestly say Albert has been my only true lifelong friend who I really miss, he was married to a lovely lady Janet and they have three beautiful daughters. I touch base with Joanne who lives in Italy and she is doing very well in the Real Estate business over there.

So back in time to the solo experiences when I moved into working 1978/1980 with another two friends of mine, sadly no longer with us too, Barry Richards and Gary Nicholls. Always great company with many a laugh along the way. But they both had much talent. Barry was a seasoned country guitar vocalist and presenter compare, who went on to own the Newbridge club in Hull together with his wife Millie. Barry who also worked abroad as I did and Gary Nicholls who had a heart of gold and an equally brilliant voice and guitarist and a fantastic artist and personality. I do so miss the regular Southern Comforts on the Tuesday shows which warmed us all up!

For what seemed a long period of time, each Monday we played Hull Elephant & Castle, Each Tuesday Hull Lambwath Hall Country club, and Hull Greenwood Hotel each Wednesday as the Kimberley's. We then split into solo gigs each Thurs/Fri/Sat/Sunday into various venues far and wide. I enjoyed this period as it gave us all a different insight into others we worked with.

For me, I was able to play bass guitar and then on my solo jobs go back to my 6-string instrument. Harmony vocalising has always interested and fascinated me. My mum actually sang in clubs on an amateur basis with my dad and could she harmonise. My mum literally showed me how with the use of octaves, and I was able to pick up this straight away. This has so much assisted my own development vocally. I find it so easy to slip into harmony lines on any song anyone might sing. My dad could play the melodeon and Accordion. My brother Howard also plays decent riffs on guitar and to this day hammers a tune out with impressive gusto on his acoustic Hoyer axe!

During 1978/79 I was able to work 2 consecutive seasons each Thursday at Wallis's Holiday Centre, Cayton Bay with Ronnie Hilton, another Hull local lad and also each Sunday at the Scarborough Futurist Minstrel Lounge through Barry Richards for which I was always so grateful for.

Another season at Sea Farm Holiday centre at Flamborough followed with Ian Anderson on keyboards and Danny on the drums. Danny and his wife ran a guest house in Bridlington too. I conducted the stage in the respect of being compere involved a few bingos/games/ theme nights we had a weekly Hawaiian evening.

The 1970's closed with more work than what could be fitted in. It certainly played havoc with my family lifestyle which was becoming a vicious circle, in that we needed money to progress in life, but I was hardly ever at home to see my children growing up and to this day I have never been able to make that time up due to the marriage break up and not wanting to sound ungrateful in any way, at that time 1987 it was not the best place to be in on matrimonial financial and child settlements as it is today.

Yes I have some regrets, but at the time as we both had new relationships I had with my very dear wife to be Julie, who has been a rock for me ever since I moved into another phase of my life story. Our first son Gareth was born in 1990 with Scott following in 1999. Gareth was particularly academic and after primary school took his place at Hull Grammar school before an amalgamation with Hull High School for girls became then being known as Hull Collegiate School. Gareth attained good exam passes at both O and A levels. He went on to attain a Law Degree at Hull University, after which Gareth commenced a 2-year training course as a Solicitor.

Gareth continued his employment by joining Rollits for a 6-year period and today works for the University of law as a Tutor teaching up and coming law students, so he has made leaps and bounds in his work ethics. Scott had a very difficult start to his life in that he had Pulmonary Atresia with VSD Ventricular Septic defect. Basically, his valves and arteries did not meet as they should, also a hole in his heart and various operations took place over the years, in fact eight in all for different essential reasons in order for him to pick up his life towards his future. Scott had what is thought to be mild stroke in an early operation which left him with right sided hemiplegia, in short, he did not have overall control of the right side of his body from the head to the toes. Bless him though as he has overcome adversity and today, he even manages to play disability football for his team Inter Barton across the river Humber from where we live.

This year 2022 was excellent for his team as they won the South Yorkshire Abilities league and he proudly stood with the trophy and the man of the match trophy. Scott is particularly good on social media and excellent at graphic work too and an excellent understanding of information Technology and currently has joined up with Beverley Town AFC who are awaiting a decision if they are to be accepted into Northern East Counties league 1 Division for next season. This development is in line with work experience through East Riding College of which he has attended for the past 6 years.

He also holds a fans media for both Hull City Supporters and Real Madrid. Previously an important opportunity for Scott occurred when a call from his consultant's secretary indicating that because of Scott's many operational procedures was there something, or somewhere, or someone to meet, or that Scott would like to go as a concession? The Starlight Foundation offer opportunities to either underprivileged or life changing procedures that children up to the age of 16 have endured, some at birth with disabilities and to grant them a wish. Scott was asked and being a football fanatic (definitely my fault) said he would like to meet Cristiano Ronaldo the world-famous footballer who plied his trade at that time in 2016 in Spain.

Just three weeks later we were on our way to Madrid. Mum, Dad (me) and Scott to be met by the wonderful Starlight Foundation team who arranged a four-night stay in a lovely central Madrid area. We were fed and watered, and they would not take one penny from us. We had an organised stadium tour at the Bernabeu and the very next day we set off for the training ground which is located close to the airport.

As the players entered for training all half dozen children from Spain and others from the UK they all signed a ball given to each of the recipients. We were then taken for food and drinks, and we sat on a balcony watching Real Madrid train for about an hour.

Each player had photos with Scott and two weeks later he was sent a photo album with all the photos to treasure for many years ahead.

It was a dream come true and all three of us are so grateful for the opportunity that we do when we can help to raise funds for this very deserving charity, which do so much to help unfortunate children.

Scott was indeed just 16 years when this occasion arose. Very lasting memories and all the family are Real Madridstas for life!

Going back slightly I did however begin to have more family time and understanding the second time around and had much more time around when we have enjoyed many wonderful occasions with my mum and dad and all of Julie's family too. We have had countless holidays especially in Jersey a place I have worked and applied business there and made many friends.

I can recall a hectic summer when we flew out of Humberside airport in 2016 to fine tune the 'Battle Of Flowers' schedule I was involved in, coming back home for a few days then flying back for the two processions in St. Helier. Malta too as I worked a lot in the 1970's, has always had a special place in my heart too and up until the early nineties we visited very regularly. I have always been very committed and fastidious to everything I have enjoyed working with, throughout my very varied careers.

CHAPTER TEN
TELEVISION & FILM WORK

I have omitted until now to mention so far of my active work I did in Films and Television work. I was a member of British Actors Equity union from 1966 until recent years.

This at that time was a requisite to be able to work in the Films industry and TV. I joined PAN ARTISTES who by and large was a small roles/cameo and Walk on Extras agency based in Sale, Cheshire, but equally very busy with work. I worked on countless episodes of Emmerdale, and I acquired small speaking roles on Coronation Street, the 'ill-fated' Albion Market soap which starred Tony Booth and Helen Shapiro (a definite teenage idol of mine growing up) of which I had just become a regular stall holder which meant sometimes 2 to 3 days work weekly on a purpose built set adjacent to Granada TV studios in Manchester.

Me as a Waiter, in Emmerdale 1990's

This soap unfortunately failed to hold a strong enough viewing audience and sadly it was curtailed, just as it was getting 'steam up' with the actors if you appreciate what I mean.

Some hilarious times abounded with 'The Sword Divided'. On a spectacular very hot summers Saturday at Belvoir Castle, Leicestershire, filming with an outdoors scene, many of us laid dead after a battle and as with many pre takes it seems to be forever that you are waiting for the scene to commence. Being laid for what appeared to be hours but possibly only 10 minutes or so, the sun burning down on us all. So, after what was an age it appeared to be a key moment when the damsel and two knights in shining armour waited patiently for the director to shout 'AND ACTION'! We had all being 'laid dead' for what seemed an eternity as I had mentioned and on action A loud snoring could be heard from one of the extras! CUT!! Shouted the director and the culprit was marched off the set, never to be seen again!

Another amusing incident at on the set of **BRIDESHEAD REVISITED** at St. Georges Hall, Liverpool brought even more devilish behaviour from a few of the 'walk on' extra artistes. A new recruit who had never worked on a set started talking with us explaining he had not done this before. (a Greenhorn or so a couple of fellow extras thought) They told the 'newbie' that you got more money if you spoke a line- 'what have they asked you to do?' they enquired of the new lad? 'Well, I have to take this tray as a waiter and they will take a glass of wine off the tray'. The person he was to take it to was none other than Sir John Gielgud. So they came to the scene and ACTION! The poor lad walked over with his tray to Sir John and retorted "SHALL I OPEN THE KERTAINS (accent for curtains) FOR YOU JOHN?"

"Cut" said the director "and get rid of that man off this set!"

We had amazing laughs but sometimes it could be quite serious. I had a speaking role as a security officer in 'Circles Of Deceit' Episode 'Kalon' with Dennis Waterman. An opening clip is visible on You Tube to this day. Now Dennis is a man of few words really and when the scene came up I asked him if he wanted a run through first? He declined and when we came to the 'Take' he fluffed his lines! Well, I did ask him, didn't I? I have just recently learned sadly that Dennis has passed away at the age of 74 in Spain. A great actor who had much success. And despite my comments it was a privilege to have worked with him.

Me in Circles of Deceit (Kalon)

I had many great days in filming, and another was 'The Nineteenth Hole' a pilot for a new sitcom about a Golf club with Eric Sykes and Norman Rossington in front of a studio audience in Nottingham. This was quite a racist programme as it definitely would have been, if cast in today's world. A full Swastika flag flew at the entrance to the Golf club to give you an insight to that meaning.

One amazing thing was the before a show the audience warm top comedian was the star of the sitcom none other than Eric Sykes who did a really fantastic job. Although a series was commissioned, a further one never materialised. Another strange one was, 'Gossip from The Forest' a film about World War 2 and the location was on Alderley Edge in Cheshire. Around 30 of us were marching through a clearing into a forestry area with a large field to the side. As we went for a practise march, we could see a farmer stood looking really puzzled seeing us all dressed in Nazi uniforms. He stopped us and said what is going on? Are we at war again? After explanations, he went on his merry way, and we shot the scene.

We did an episode of that sitcom 'Common as Muck' on a council estate in Oldham. The scene was to be a funeral cortege from one of the houses and I spent a really interesting afternoon with the actor Edward Woodward. When we all came out of the house for the take people were out and about in their hundreds. It took an hour to shut them up, in the end they brought in an ice cream van and parked a block away and gave them all free ice creams to quell the noise.

Another funny episode was on Coronation Street. The caterers who supplied the food all day had brought in a single decker bus with seats and tables so you could get your food and take it onto the bus to eat. Charlie Lawson who plays Jim McDonald walks into the bus with his fry up and sits down. "Has anyone got the salt?" he bellowed. I passed him ours from the table. He grabbed and turned it onto his meal and the whole of the salt cellar exploded onto his food! Needless to say, the language was not for the faint hearted! But everyone fell about laughing!

Lots of rare locations too. I once had to meet at Leeds station for a trip to Kings Cross, London. The plot was football fans fighting. Luckily, I was sat at a table reading the Times when a fight was staged next to me, this continued through 12 takes and some people ended up with severe bruising and worse. Well as stunt performers they can expect some rough and tumble. Once in London we had to wait as several more scenes were filmed by the side of the station then again when we took the return train more fighting ensued as part of the plot. I believe we commandeered three carriages for the filming. I had a speaking role in Heartbeat playing the part of Dennis Parker. In the scene were most of the police characters Nick, Ventress, Bellamy, Blaketon and Kate. The part was small but took us 2 days to complete due to different scenes in the storyline. To this day I still have the original hard copy script.

I took part in some 'Walk On' scenes in different episodes with Otley market doubling for Whitby bus station. Another opportunity on heartbeat saw me face to face with 'old Greengrass'. (Bill Maynard a lovely man may I say) and his trusted canine and I was able to recall meeting up with his son some years previous whilst on tour. Another Soap I worked on was Brookside which saw me as a forensic on the 'body under the patio' scene, which was watched by record numbers of viewers apparently, we were told. Brookside was a soap that I had expected to have run forever pretty much like Corrie, but it was not to be.

In more recent times I had the pleasure of a couple of scenes in the feature film 'Everyone's

Talking About Jamie' which was primarily filmed in Sheffield. This I believe is on Prime video as it failed to hit the Cinemas in a big way due to the pandemic closures of all hospitality cinema outlets. I made great friends with an Asian guy who had the main speaking role in his corner shop. It was a good scene and we waded through our bit in just two takes. To this day because of the pandemic even though lots of money had been thrown at this production it never was able to be shown at cinemas and to the best of my knowledge it was shown on Prime Video but I have never seen it myself to this day.

In summary on filming, it often played havoc with evening shows as you never really know when the director will call a WRAP for the days shooting. So it was often a mad dash to be able to get to the venue to perform my musical talents because of the uncertainty of the finish times when filming during the day shoots.

In a situation working on a period drama at Blackpool Tower Ballroom we did a full day's shoot and on the way home I was called by my agent to return the next day as they had found what is known as a 'Hair In The Gate' which in simple terms is that a hair had worked its way inside the camera lens outwardly and in the old filming the only way to get shut of that was to re shoot the whole work that was affected. This never happens today as the techniques used do not encompass these problems that did occur previously.

A great opportunity occurred for me as a 'Stunt' man. The shooting took place in Ancotes, a favoured area for the artist LS Lowry, in Manchester. I was asked to double with the Irish actor Tony O'Doyle on the final shot of the popular series 'BAND OF GOLD'. The lady that played Sam on action slit my throat- well not really and I had a blood all over me in the cochineal mixed with a sugary substance from my neck downwards. I had to crawl through real glass and lay with my head against a Jaguar vehicle and that scene closed the series. For me though it was the beginning. I was in such a mess I was driven back to the Granada TV Studios for a shower, a big clean up as my underclothes were ruined. The wardrobe found some suitable clothes for me before I could walk away and back to my car for the journey home. I still have some stills that feature in the book photos. The strange thing was that walking through the corridors to tidy myself up I almost bumped into Cilla Black who retorted 'My God are you ok?' We did however have many freezing cold days when we had to keep ourselves warm, especially out on locations, when it was a complete outdoor shoot.

Final take, 'BAND OF GOLD'

The Siege at Home Farm, Emmerdale

Chief Forensic, Brookside (Body Under the Patio)

We always get fed and watered and the good days and nights far outweighed the bad. In one year I worked 45 days on various shoots as either a walk on extra /cameos or small parts which I thoroughly enjoyed.

The first ever time I did a film shoot however was at Leeds Town Hall with a French version of the Charles Dickens novel 'A Tale of Two Cities' a cast of many people had to greet a coach and horses on the steps of the Town Hall. The French, very recognisable for their love of wine, drafted in crate loads of the stuff into the catering area.

This was a two session film shoot, but it was to be overnight filming and at feeding time so many of the extras got absolutely plastered with the drink. Needless to say after several had been dismissed from the set due to being worse the wear to say the least, the production team banned all wine for the second nights shoot.

It was there I first met the wonderful Elaine and Johnny Jackson (an amazing and very funny twosome) a top clubland act plying their trade in Northern clubs and venues, but with us for filming on these two overnight shoots. Now, Johnny told me one evening at a club at Kellingley Social centre they were announced on stage... The first part of their rehearsed act was to open with a song with Johnny singing totally out of tune. But halfway through this song the chairman went up to his box and shut the curtains and announced to the audience he was 'paying them off' now the term 'paying an act off' was due to 'in the concert chairman's opinion' the act was not good enough to continue with their act. Now Johnny and Elaine rounded up on the chairman to say that it was part of the act to sing out of tune, but oh no! the chairman was having none of it and they walked out of the venue with a tenner expenses only for their cheek as he put it!

I caught up several times with Elaine in the late 80's as she resides in the city I live in too when she visited a residency I was working at that time. It was often thought that club committee men (never a lady in sight or allowed on a committee in those days) had the notion that an act received financially, for one performance, what the working men and many were coal miners got for a week's hard graft! This was often frowned upon, but it is really down to the fact that not one of the punters in the club could entertain. Horses for courses might be a term to use? The killer for me was that even though you would tell the concert chairman who would introduce the act not to do so until you gave him the thumbs up, but they just never listened to that request. As soon as you stepped on to the 'hallowed boards' they would introduce you. Well ok if you are a comedian but for me and various people, I ever worked on stage with that had equipment to switch on guitars to put over your head checking all was ready to entertain it could be a nightmare.

One of the most difficult things was that if I had an evening's engagement it was always a worry what time we would get a 'WRAP call to end the day's filming proceedings as I have already indicated previously. Many last minute dashes to arrive minutes before taking to the stage. However I managed this at times I will never know!

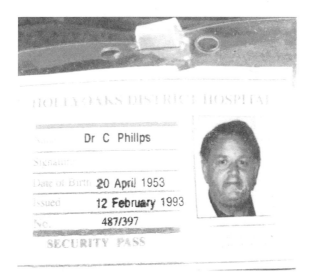

HOLLYOAKS DISTRICT HOSPITAL

	Dr C Phillps
Stefanie	
Date of Birth	20 April 1953
Issued	12 February 1993
No.	487/397

SECURITY PASS

My Dr. Security Badge when I was an extra
for 3 episodes of Hollyoaks.

CHAPTER ELEVEN

DISCO DAVE!

By the mid 1990's it became apparent that live music was turning a corner. In as much that for the late 1970's artistes relied on their own backing but karaoke in the mid 80's from Japan had finally taken a hold in the UK and backing tracks were invented. The problem was they made them up as cassettes. But these often did not work as they were meant to. The tapes often got baffled up or having played one side through it meant if you forgot to wind back you had to begin all over again. This had not been thought through and I for one refused to get involved.

A friend of mine was a DJ so I thought 'right I know a thing or three about music' so here comes 'DJ Dave'.

I obtained some extra equipment, I obviously had a fair amount from all my live music days, so with CD's taking to the fore I started my collection of 'NOW That's What I Call Music' CD's. I eventually worked for a decent outfit in Disco date who got me up and running with work and they supplied most of the equipment to deliver the sound and I just had to use my discs.

I played a long residency at The Corn Mill Hotel in Hull and had some wonderful nights under the watchful eye of Clive Briglin (Disco date) and Jack Crooks the Hotel General Manager. I must have worked around 3 years or so and almost went to Jeddah in Saudi Arabia as a gig had come up. I believe visas were an issue and it just didn't quite materialise for me to fly out there.

Disco date with Steve Ryan at the helm proved a good steppingstone in my entertainment days. I only ever had an issue with Colin Conman of Alan Ford discos who was for me not as straight up and down as he should have been with his employees, especially in a financial way. That said, enough of that experience. I also at that time played a fortnightly Wednesday evening at the Merchant Navy Hotel in Hull for the manager Vic Holgate who was a lovely elderly person, and he ran a very tight ship putting shows on for single and divorced individuals to help get their lives back on track with possible new partners. This gig went on for several years and became a great part of my entertainment life.

As time marched on taped backing tracks gave way to Mini discs and so it became much easier to operate the backing tracks without hitting playback issues. I applied and was given the comperes job at the Lawns Club in Sutton-On-

Hull and worked the venue for around a two-year period. I really, looking back, used this as a stepping stone to ease my way back onto the live music scene, but in doing so I made a lot of new friends. Jack and Maureen Riley ran the establishment and were as fair a team that you could wish to work for. Old Cyril on the door became a firm friend as did all the guests that I came to know and love throughout that period. I did however also do short periods of residency at Suttonway club for Tony Riley and Capper Pass social clubs as a rest period from touring the country.

CHAPTER TWELVE
FAST FORWARD

In total I have worked in the business some 59 years nearing my 60th year in 2023. In more recent times I have had the pleasure in promoting a few UK tours and also promoting artistes on the island of Jersey in the Channel Islands.

I met Jackie and Alan Donald who are an inspirational couple who have been involved in the 'Battle of Flowers' organisation and planning. Jackie was the events director who steered the 'Battle of Flowers' Committee. This event is an annual display of flowers on floats made up of various themes such as Mary Poppins or 101 Dalmatians and so on.

This exceptional procession has been organised since the early 20th century and a lot of work is put into the floats prior who represent all of the States of Jersey. The States of Jersey are made up of all the areas, for instance we have St. Helier, St. Clement, St. Peter, Trinity, Grouville, St. Brelade, St. John, St.Lawrence, St. Martin, St. Mary, St. Saviour, and St. Ouen. Twelve states in all with most of them submitting entries each years.

I must add that most years 'The Optimists' often presented the best float year after year. Now each year a special float with an elected Miss Battle and Mr Battle with the Mr Battle who has traditionally been a celebrity. I have had the pleasure of organising Mr. Battle on non-other than 5 occasions including 2011 Gareth Gates, 2012 Matthew Wolfenden, 2013 Mikey North, 2014 Ray Quinn, 2015 Craig Phillips, and 2016 Joe McElderry. The floats have a daytime procession and a moonlight parade the following evening. Many people from all over the world visit for this momentous occasion on this wonderful UK Island.

I was asked by Ray Quinn's Manager Steve Coxshall to arrange a UK tour which I duly did. A lot of toil and sweat is involved in putting tours together, but enjoyable all the same.

Ray himself was a very amenable person who had gone on from his success on X factor to TV'S 'Dancing on Ice' which he eventually won an overall winners show, after which until 2014 he decided to return to singing. For himself he wanted to work the big arenas again but with an 8-year gap or so many of his fans had married and had families of their own, he found it more difficult to maintain his previous massive popularity and although he released another swing type album it did not give him the recognition he surely deserved.

If Ray had done something more original vocally, as he sang really well, it may have helped him as Swing was big at the time, but Michael Bublé was the star of swing at that point and to me that had already been done. Ray and his Manager parted company a few months later and he by his own talents is now making his way as a seasoned actor and vocalist and his talent continues to shine through in musicals and the like as well as personal show performances. Ray will always be in work as his talents go before him.

I Went down to the 'Rabbit Hole' in London on a couple of occasions to finalise tour details and to check out the London venue he worked twice on that particular tour. Organising tours really does test anyone's resolve. Such an enormous amount of calls, emails, and overall planning and a full tour can take months to prepare.

CHAPTER THIRTEEN

THE WHISTLE BLOWER?

Well not in the same vein and a period in my life back pedalling during 1989 when with my great interest in football and it was really through my brother Howard who was really becoming a very competent match official himself. Howard a class 1 referee officiated in outside leagues and competently achieving top success himself with the whistle. It was because of my brother I decided to take up the whistle and duly sat my Class 3 exam which I managed to attain.

My wife Julie pregnant with our forthcoming first Son Gareth, came to meet me on the night that I passed the exam. I continued and was able due to my semi-professional take in entertainment to find space on a Saturday/Sunday to referee at a local level of which I then was assessed and after a short time assessed through to Class 2 and then by exam to Class 1. At class 1 I was too old to progress to the outside leagues so achieved a good standard by refereeing leading amateur leagues and also the Northern Intermediate league which had the younger junior players of many of the Northern Football league clubs.

These games were mainly played at the local BP Ground at Saltend, Hull, and usually on a Saturday morning. By chance I was given a few games refereeing Hull Schoolboys and also East Riding Schoolboys and a particular English Schools Shield tie between East Riding and Nottingham at under 15 level. For East Riding in goal was a future star Paul Robinson and for Nottingham none other than Jermaine Pennant who again became a massive name in the premier league.

After the game a gentleman I later found out was Jack Tarr, who was a selector at National level for referees for English schoolboys, approached me and asked if I had enjoyed the match as a referee. I said it had been a pleasure and looked forward to doing more similar games. Mr Tarr told me he thought I had handled the game well and asked if I would like to referee some matches for the English Schools in the future. I agreed and before long I had some Schools matches that took me all over Lincolnshire, Yorkshire, and Lancashire.

I was lucky enough to be appointed to be a referee's assistant at an international England v Wales game, played at Scunthorpe in 1998, England v Scotland Victory Shield, played at Nottingham Forest in 1997 and the pinnacle was an appointment to referee the England v Holland under 18 match at Wembley in 1999. I was also lucky enough to referee county cup semi-finals and finals and forever grateful for Jack and his team of refereeing assessors.

It is a question really of being at the right place at the right time. No matter how good you are you do need that bit of 'good luck' to make progress as I fortunately did. It was at a local referees evening that a very genial and funny guy by the name of Frank Broughton delivered the funniest gag I think I ever heard! So it goes...

"A couple, we will call them George and Betty, had just got married and they went to North America for their 'Honeymoon' they stayed at a remote hotel in the far reaches of Montana.

They came down to breakfast and on the notice board they noted 'A trip to an Indian Reservation' George said to his new wife shall we go? So they booked and, on the day, they took the two hour drive and half an hour on foot when they came to a clearing with all the tepees before them. But on top of one of the tepees was a notice stating 'THE INDIAN MEMORY MAN' I can answer any question that you put to me. George said to Betty shall we go in, he will not have a clue, his wife said what do you mean? He said, "You will soon see..." His wife agreed and they stepped into the tepee and they're standing before them was the thinnest Indian you had ever saw with 1 feather in his headband. So George said to the Indian 'who won the Scottish cup in 1871? The Indian said in broad American twang well Rangers beat Patrick Thistle one nil. Well neither could believe this! An Indian in the

144

middle of 'nowhere' answering a question on football going back so far.

After the honeymoon and when they arrived back home, he told all his mates, and they couldn't believe it either. But 25 years passed, and the couple decided to relive their honeymoon and revisit the same hotel in North America.

On coming down for breakfast George said Hey that trip to the Indian reservation is still on shall we go? Betty said yes, we must! They booked and took the two-hour trip, half an hour on foot, and came to the clearing where the tepees were. But the Indian memory man with one feather in his headband had become the 'Big Chief' of the village with masses of feathers everywhere.

His wife said you had better show some respect when we go in. George said, 'yes I will' As they entered the tepee he went up and raising his hand and said to the Indian HOW! The Indian said, 'A Penalty In The 89th Minute'!!!

Just love that punch line! How good was that? Since writing the above I actually met up with

Frank at a football final at the MKM Stadium and I told him the joke he told many moons ago. He is in his eighties, and he could not remember delivering this at all. However we recalled some good times and Ian Blanchard thought the gag had some promise for one of his own referee talks he often gives to different audiences within the area we live.

Another little story here. My wife and eldest son Gareth accompanied me to the Wembley match May 1999 when we travelled down to London and stayed at the Harrow Quality Hotel for the pre match rally meal on the Friday night. Come the following day Jack had taken a liking to my son Gareth (he was 9 years at the time) and asked him if he would accompany the match officials to the changing rooms and carry out the match balls before the game.

Whilst this was going on my wife and the other officials' wives were trying to find the gate to let them into the old twin towers at Wembley Stadium. After walking all the way around twice they stopped an official to ask where they should enter the ground. This official looked at the tickets and said no wonder you cannot find your entrance you are going into the Royal Box!

Well back into the changing rooms and eventually we all trooped out with the players pre match Gareth brought out the balls and he made his way up to the Royal Box afterwards the same steps many famous players had walked throughout the years the stadium had been used for football since 1923. The day was living the dream! The match went well, and we were treated to a wonderful afternoon tea at the end of the match enjoyed by us all. A big thank you to Jack and the English school's team of organisers and back up the A1 to pinch ourselves that was it surely not reality, or was it? I still to this day referee small, sided games but on a much lower level. I have some lovely trophies I still treasure to this day gained through my interest and lucky success I was fortunate to have in the sport.

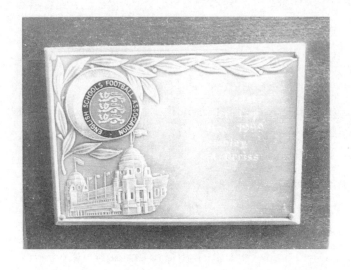

England V Holland U18's at Wembley May 1999
- Referee Plaque

It is a great networking sport to be connected with, but you also need that luck to be spotted and invited to participate at this high level as I had previously indicated. Further to this I had the pleasure of refereeing two matches in Malta during 1993, one at Ta'Qali National Stadium and one at Hibernians ground at Paola near Valletta. The main stadium game featured Valletta v Hamrun Spartans.

The facilities in Malta had been very well developed and at that time was definitely a 'state-of-the-art' in stadium and training facilities. The game went fine. I had two experienced assistants running the line and corporate hospitality to all of us officials and were given a lovely tea after the match was completed.

The hospitality by the Maltese was second to none and I looked forward to the second match at Hibernians in Paola Valletta. The match at Hibernians v Floriana took place two days later. Again, they could not do enough for me.

In contrast to the English game I did find that tempers flew around quite unnecessarily at times, whereas these local referees took tolerance to the limit, I had to take action on some silly challenges and robust play and antics, but overall an enjoyable experience and my thanks were sent over to Mr. J Lolley the referees' appointments secretary for this rare opportunity.

I did in 1998 begin a chapter at Hull City looking after the Match officials giving corporate hospitality at Boothferry Park. This opportunity occurred during a brief word from Rob Smith, he himself was a good footballer, but was involved with administrative duties, especially on home match days and he invited me to look after the match officials on home match days. I gratefully accepted the offer which had previously been held by Freddie Barr who had decided to retire from this duty he had held for some years.

I continued this great opportunity in 2002 when we transferred to the brand new K Com Stadium built within the West Park area of the city and on the spot where the 'Circle' cricket ground had stood for many years and a part of the old Hull City Anlaby road ground of which I had the pleasure of being a member of one of the last teams to ever play on this 'hallowed' ground before a railway line was built through the centre of the pitch.

This was a shield final between Alderman Cogan old boys and Fish Trades, and we won the game 4-2 and my boss of the bakery I worked at the time was Bob Mcleish was amongst the official guests at that memorable evening. Obviously, the old stands had disappeared, but the pitch was still in use from time to time and what wonderful memories for me as I had begun to collect such rare pre-war Hull City programmes and painted a 'mind's eye' picture of maybe how it used to be all those years back.

In total I have been connected with Hull City AFC now for 24 years coming on to my 25th year next year 2023, so here's hoping! I have met some of the best referees in the world including Howard Webb, Mark Clattenburg, Stuart Attwell, Kevin Friend, Anthony Taylor, Andre Marriner and perhaps my most respected officials were Mark Clattenburg, Howard Webb, Mark Halsey and Lee Mason. With Lee we even used to do singing duets in the refs room and good craic was the order of the day on his every visit. Mark Halsey was just a lovely, lovely man who epitomised what all referees' should aspire to.

Me as Referee, Hull City Programme Feature

Unfortunately, some were not so versed in the man management areas and stuck solidly to 'the laws of the game' and very evident in my refereeing career as if you had a job as a teacher or a policeman these were the areas of employment that seemed to make their way into refereeing.

For some it meant because of their background they were able to carry the games well, but for others they often steamrolled their way over fellow officials which to me was autocratic and well out of date.

Cliques of referees at every level occurred believe me, but I always felt more at home when meeting some of the refs with more working-class backgrounds such as Mark Clattenburg who basically called a 'spade a spade' and took no 'airs and graces.' I worked with greats such as Uriah Rennie, one name off the top of my head, but regardless every one of these officials hold a special place in my heart for one reason or another it's just they all have a varied take on what was necessary to carry out the duties as a match official.

So in reiteration after my normal 11 a side retirement from refereeing and as mentioned above, I was invited by Rob Smith who was an employee at the time (and previously no mean footy player himself) at Hull City AFC to have the opportunity of taking over from Freddie Barr (a former football league referee) as he had retired from this position which was to give corporate hospitality to the visiting match officials at each home game as Referee Liaison officer. This was in 1998 and so began a long association with the club and game I both loved.

At Boothferry Park it was difficult to give other than cups of tea/ coffee pre and post-match and biscuits and if lucky some sausage rolls to the officials. Several interesting episodes over the Boothferry Park days happened as in this instance, Rotherham United's, Guy Branston - a player who had been sent off by the match day referee, steamrolled his way and came into the ref's area and smashed his fist through a plate glass window that led to the referee's room. Stupidly he put his fist through the glass, and he then retracted his hand back which was against the grain of the glass and very nearly severed an artery but fortunately at each game an ambulance is present and First Aiders were at hand to rush him to hospital for treatment and an overnight stay at the Hull HRI.

Another but a more amusing incident was that I was making a large pot of tea for the officials and my location was directly below the main stand. Suddenly a massive eruption of cheering saw me drop the tea pot with tea all over me! It was because a home team goal had been scored and the massive noise startled me!

Over the years I wrote a job description and in my absence my brother Howard often stood in for me. Howard was a very successful football referee plying his trade in the North-Eastern Counties outside leagues for many years and so was an ideal stand in for myself on such occasions.

By 2001 and still enjoying this part time involvement with the game and team I loved, our new stadium the K Com stadium opened at the Circle which backed onto Hull's West Park area. We enjoyed many, many wonderful occasions, the stadium manager John Cooper had a wealth of experience on pitches, man management and carried on from his Boothferry Park days and was the man at the helm until the late 2000 teen years overseeing England representative games, Europa Cup games after our promotion to the Premier league.

I myself met many, many players and celebrities, top class referees and assistants who always had time for what I was able to offer them as visitors on match days. it was such a pleasure to meet Bobby Charlton and state what a pleasure it was to meet him. He said in return 'it is a pleasure to meet you' me a nobody really in the company of such a great man realising how humble he was with those lovely words back. A man I do and will always hold in the highest esteem. The staff turnover each season really astounded me. It would seem that some just disappeared, some left to pursue other careers but this to me left a void so that inconsistency of management and staff training alike, deteriorated at times and decisions were made that for me was often in conflict with past needs and requirements. So much so that the then club owners failed in man- management issues.

The new security manager decided to weed out who he didn't either want or like in his new domain as the boss. One by one certain staff in the players areas either left or went to other positions in hospitality by his hand. He brought in some individuals I would not employ sweeping up never mind employ in security! I certainly fell foul of this person in that for some reason one match day he told me to position myself in an area that was not my domain. However, it is water under the bridge and although I was livid at the time it was no time to dwell as I have a great relationship with Hull City AFC and they soon found a lovely hospitality position for me which I do so much enjoy to this day.

My area was always in and out of the referees' changing areas and positioning outside the main referee doors' entrances. However, this particular day I was positioned next to the entrance to the outside corridor. A referee came along this corridor, and it was good to see my referee pal by the name of Kevin Friend, a Premier Elite Referee, a person who I had known for a long period of time. He had arrived by chance to watch the match and needed a ticket. Although this new security 'head honcho' said that people or persons unknown to me shall not pass through into this so-called sterile area, as he was not unknown to me and (not a threat to anyone) I duly took Kevin through to see the club secretary's assistant, who duly gave him a ticket and I took him back and wished him well.

This 'head honcho' sent me an 'e-mail' telling me he did not want me in this area again? WHAT! I have never stepped out of line and the mere fact that I had spent over 21 years in this position validates this. I hold a current SIA badge licence. (Security Industry Authority) so I am publicly aware of what is needed from myself.

The new security employee apparently failed to possess any man management skills whatsoever and it was more than obvious he wanted his own choice of people working under him. I could never forgive him and never will as he acted in an unfair way letting me know he didn't want me by his treatment and being sent a 'bloody' e-mail to inform me of this! What sort of a peoples' person was he ever schooled at? I find treatment like this abhorrent, I wrote to the owners about this disparaging way of moving me out of the area. They were just as impossible to deal with too, as they never had the decency to even reply! Another peoples' persons failure! As owners they did not have one ounce of consideration for anyone but themselves.

This was a case of disgusting treatment from two different individuals who had not the balls to tell me face to face, and by the way had I done anything wrong? Many people at the club agreed with me, but I failed to get vital backing from the nearest I had worked with for years either. So in a nutshell my own thoughts are that sports clubs could and should be run a lot smoother than they currently do.

I have never been in an employment with such a massive turnover of staff, both player wise, administrative wise and stewarding! It is the club I love and care for more than anything, but it would have been so much simpler if it had been more family oriented from the top at that period of time. As I write this, I do believe we are moving into a much more understanding of staff needs and truly hope this continues.

After looking after these officials I still to this day, as mentioned, work in hospitality at Hull City with really excellent colleagues such as Les Cammish, Tony Normington and Brian Goodrick who I work closely with other good colleagues Ron, Gary, Pat and Maureen, Karen,

Harry, Helen, Robyn, Luke, Paul, and others. And indeed all people I come across in my daily duties, with a mention of Ann Holland who looks after disabilities welfare needs of the spectators and does a really wonderful job indeed.

Ann is a fab 'peoples' person' liked by everyone. At the newly named **MKM** Stadium, new owners mean exciting possibilities. We welcome Acun Ilicali to our beloved club and his background team. As I write this, we have maintained our presence in the Championship for next season 2022/23 and very excited at what we might be able to achieve in the forthcoming season.

CHAPTER FOURTEEN
A BRIDGE TOO FAR?

Work became a daytime necessity again I applied and after an interview was taken on at the largest suspension bridge in the world, the Humber Bridge as a part time bridge assistant.

It was the last day for submitting an application and I drove with Julie to hand in my application at the Hessle Job centre one Friday afternoon in May 1998. I always believed that I managed to obtain an interview as I noticed that in place was a box full of applications and mine went on to the top.

To this day I truly believe I was given an interview because my application must have had an early perusal because of the timing and positioning of the application form. I got along very well with the Chief Inspector John Oxley from the beginning. We both had similar interests, football for one and I refereed several tournaments for the local Barton Town teams where he held good contacts.

I managed to progress to a full-time day shift as a Bridge Officer and even took on, for a time, a three shift working system to enhance my wages. I was lucky enough to have a presentation limited edition plaque given to me and my good colleague John Hill and other bridge officers and administration staff were given these mementoes on the occasion of the 25th anniversary of the bridge opening.

Work on the bridge continued for me for 12 years but sadly the way the bridge operated was often very sloppy at times and as a union representative for the Bridge officers I had several run ins with the Bridge Master Peter Hill over various discrepancies.

Unfortunately, a certain arrogant John Williams (not the famed musician by the way) tried to disrupt various employees and like Peter Hill is now no longer part of the set up. Surprise, surprise!

I hear it's even worse now though! Cannot go down that track as I know 'Na'thing'!!

Another interesting facet was the arrival of a film crew with Jeremy Clarkson from 'Top Gear' fame and who later on stepped into Chris Tarrant's shoes on 'Who Wants To Be A Millionaire?'

One of our Bridge officers Mark Walton (although he was aware of his visit) disliked Clarkson intently and a request from the production team 'that could one of the Bridge officers take a seat in the latest vehicle being shown crossing the bridge with Jeremy driving? So, the plan was set, and Mark was told he was needed to take his place in the rear seat of a test car.

Imagine his shock to find Jeremy had arrived to take him on a ride! He took it all in good heart though in this new vehicle and waved to us all as he passed! What a day that was! Another crazy episode involved a certain lady, yes Debbie a Bridge officer who was real fun and a likeable person, but to quote a saying, 'Had a mouth like a Foghorn' nothing wrong in that, but the following maybe had given her that title.

I had just departed from my booth for a break when Debbie a Bridge officer in her booth shouted in a very loud decibel, 'Hey Dave!! The vehicle that had departed her lane screeched to a halt and the next car following crashing into the rear of the departing car. What's up said the front driver only to be told by Debbie "I was only shouting after a colleague of mine!"

Never did find out any further information on that incident though.

Most of the staff were very likeable, amiable and great characters and we tended to back each other as issues did mount from time to time. With the inspectors and some of the supervisors were at times super critical and some acted with having little peoples skills, although a great story was that a bridge officer brought in a contraption which looked remarkably like a possible bomb, found on a vehicle patrol from a site on the south bank anchorage area; but instead of radioing this to the control tower he took the item physically and up to the control room!!

Thankfully it was not a bomb and as recognition for bringing the suspect contraption to the control room, he was promoted, and he eventually became an inspector! The things you have to achieve to be recognised...

Great people though at the bridge including Jane Jacklin, John Hill, Dean Cummings and Sandy Beacock, now like Dean, they departed due to the backward changes in my opinion - of making the shifts into 12 hours!

That is not a step forward and the people that decided on this change will never have to work those ridiculous hours themselves.

Richard Sedman, Dave Gibbs, Bob Huntley, Martin Bremner and also Roy Uzzell who became a good friend - often went to Hull City away games together. Likewise, Paul and Debbie Clipson (yes, they met at the 'Bridge' and tied the knot eventually!) and so many more lovely people who worked over the years that I was employed there.

Paul and I went to Nashville to see the Country Music Awards in around 2006. He was always good company and lots of laughs and joking when he was around, as were Sandy Beacock and Mick Rendell who were such characters in their own right.

CHAPTER FIFTEEN

THE EAST COAST AS A PROMOTER & AGENT DEALINGS

As the years progressed, I began to take an interest in promoting shows myself. Not just for me but to promote other fine acts especially from our own region.

Also, at times I disagreed with the way agents were conducting themselves towards the artistes they had on their books 'so called' represented acts.

I say this because in contacting several well-known and reasonably respected agents over the years and as an up-and-coming Roy Orbison tribute act, I felt there was a lot of opportunity to be able to work regularly in this mode. However, some of the feedback from agents was, 'Well we are not being asked for a Roy Orbison tribute.'

My take on this was short and sharp. 'Well it's up to you as an agent to earn your dough and push every one of the tributes. 'You have been given the tools, then be an agent and work to help the act as well as yourself.'

In other words, get off your 'bums' and work for your clients, as without the artistes you have no position as an agent.

These days, agents also have the habit of giving a list of tributes to the venues instead of pushing them and earning their respect. I have nothing against them plying their trade, but for *goodness sake* please act and represent these artistes and as though you have some care for them and not your own self esteem by leaving it to the venue to decide.

One Promoter I came across was Chris Woods from Selby. Chris gave me some work at Whitby Pavilion purveying my Del Shannon tribute show. An afternoons half hour slot which went down as well as I could imagine. Chris also put me into Bridlington Spa Royal Hall (the larger venue on

site) for a Roy Orbison half hour during a
Saturday afternoon show.

Me as Roy Orbison

Chris always put the tribute acts on in the
afternoon followed by mainly live 60's groups
that still had the odd member or so representing
previous hit parading groups of the past. It was
never going to be 'mega bucks' as Chris had that

many acts on the whole show day and night that it became an expenses gig on show for the patron's future consideration only. To me, Chris is one of the good guys.

Some Promoters rule the roost, so as to speak, and very much like some of the Tour Managers that operate UK tours.

Recently during the 2020 pandemic it has been notable at the worries they do carry though, because if any of the shows' cast contracted covid then the show or even the tour could be curtailed.

However, I have been side-tracked...

Before, at that time, I organised a meet up with the best and most wonderful person I have ever worked with in business and promotions, did we sing from the same hymn sheet? Of that there is no doubt. I.E. Tracey Wilson the Manager at the Hornsea Floral Hall. This venue was literally on the sea front and had been built before the war as an entertainment's venue.

We had meetings to discuss my ideas of organising concerts throughout the summer months especially during the school holidays with Cabaret and tribute evenings. We set ticket fees and Tracey was very helpful networking these shows. I utilised local Radio and postering around the town and caravan parks and local villages and of course on Facebook and other media outlets that were just taking off at that time.

Now Hornsea is a lovely town but 'very parochial indeed' in its approach which in my meaning, was that if you put tickets on at £10 they would say HOW MUCH?

So, a little tweaking and we usually put the tickets out at £5 per head or a family of 4 for £18 and so on. We often gave free raffle tickets as well as pricing them. We had very generous donors for raffle prizes, and I always supplied a good array of prizes myself. We always had advance publicity on forthcoming shows which we gave to each patron as they entered for that evening's particular show. So in other words Tracey got on with her job and I did mine.

Advance sales were always good as Tracey really worked hard at her end of the promotion and on top of that it was usual for a 'walk up' on the evening as many were on holiday which usually gave us good audiences for every show.

In the summer we ran 10-12 shows with one on most weekends and sometimes two. This arrangement lasted some 4-5 years until Tracey decided to retire from the position to settle down with her husband Glenn for some quality time together. It was never the same again at the glorious Floral Hall. I always booked in top talent.

For instance, we booked Ian Houghton from Skegness who sounded and looked more than Gene Pitney than the real one did himself. Mark Barrie from Greater Manchester and impressions of Frankie Valli and Barry Gibb of the Bee Gees.

Mark made the final of 'Stars In Their Eyes' TV production and locally myself and the fantastic Billy Summers whose impression of Billy Fury had to be seen to be believed.

Billy worked many shows at the Floral Hall and I can say our joint tribute renditions and then our finale set with sixties Rock 'N' Roll always left them wanting more and they are still talked about now when I visit Hornsea for days out. We had country music evenings additionally this being an area of music I covered of which I will mention later on.

Darren Busby perhaps was the leading country music artiste which always guaranteed to fill the house!

Eventually the Floral Hall could no longer sustain itself financially and the East Riding council decided they would pull it down and turn it into a car park. What a bad idea that surely was!? Because of this, a local committee was formed and in their negotiations with the council it was decided with financial assistance over a fixed period of time they could eventually run it as a voluntary business, with hierarchy (directors) who would take it onto the next level.

They did however for a while, take on a paid manager but this did not appear to work and so the Cafe and Hall went on to be managed as before by the voluntary sector of which for a 2 year period or so I became involved, but did not carry on shows as higher rentals of the venue became an issue and as we all have to benefit, I stepped down from show promoting.

To this day the venue seems to be functioning ok, but shows have never appeared as before in the abundance that we had under Tracey.

As well as the Floral Hall, I promoted shows at Bridlington Spa Theatre successfully. On promoting you have to have your wits about you, especially negotiating terms with the venue. I normally attempted to achieve an 80/20% split in my favour but sometimes it was 70/30% in my favour sometimes 60/40%. Hiring the venue was not a good idea as the venue did not put any effort in selling tickets that way. As long as they had a financial input it generally worked. There was always a lot of work to design and produce posters, Radio/TV to promote, news media to contact and generally attending the venue on the evening always helped.

I promoted twice a much-loved UK country favourite in Charlie Landsborough, a national name in the genre of UK country music. However, it was the only area I lost money as Charlie's Manager Ken needed a set high fee for Charlie to turn out to perform.

Ken being a very reasonable gent offset an amount to help me out, of which I was forever grateful for. I also promoted a great Cliff Richard tribute in the name of Jimmy Jemain and his Knight Shadows band graced the stage in another successful show at this fine Bridlington theatre. Jimmy also headlined for me at Hornsea Floral Hall too.

Charlie through his manager Ken organised a regional choir competition which saw both of my sons, Gareth and Scott becoming involved. The Hull Choral Union Junior Choir won through to appear at Bridlington Spa before one of Charlie's concerts - with our sons, Gareth on keyboards and Scott a choir member, appeared singing one of Charlie's self-written songs, 'Your Special You Know' superbly conducted by Gabrielle Awre who spent many hours coaching the junior members at that time.

I have promoted other shows at the Bridlington Spa including 'The Starstruck Show' with myself, Billy Summers (Billy Fury) Vic Baulton (Star comedian) and Mike Carter (Top Impressionist) and Mark Barrie (tribute). This ran for a short season several times during the 2012 summer.

Also, Ray Quinn played this venue as part of the UK Tour I promoted in 2016. A few years earlier I had the pleasure of joining up with a few acts who purveyed their tributes, and we formed together a show in which I worked alongside the wonderful John Daniels with his Frank Sinatra and fellow rat pack artistes Rat Pack Dean Martin, Sammy Davis Jnr, Becky Brown with her interpretation of Brenda Lee and a few others that made up the show in which we did local venues.

Unfortunately, a very small number of individuals suffer from a disease that no surgeon in the world has ever bottomed and cured. Is this a surprise to any of you?

The disease is called... **JEALOUSY!** I have many people I endear to.

I pride myself as being very much a people's person but have come across a few individuals who no matter how close you try to become to them, they react in a dis respectful and often, in an unruly way.

No names, no pack drill, but one such individual was assisting my eldest Son in a rehearsal at a local club. We set up my speakers to assist to a respectable volume for his violin piece, he was rehearsing for a show he was to be involved in at the Hull New Theatre. At one point a loud upturn in volume - operated by the individual culprit concerned, on the amplification caused the speakers to blow and a tidy £500 was needed to pay for the cones to be replaced in the speakers. It was not the cash to pay that upset me, but to have whom I thought was 'a so-called friend', who thought he was an expert on using sound systems to be involved to cause this to occur. I could not believe, never mind being able to forgive!

Sadly, this same individual did exactly the same thing a few weeks later, and my repair guy could not believe that 3 sets of speakers had been damaged in such a short period of time.

I should have realised what was happening, but you put your trust in a so-called friend who really was not that at all or was he just naive on how to handle sound systems? I can assure you - he knew what he was doing.

This increase in volume which would eventually blow any speaker happened at a live performance in Leeds and other venues when this person attended with me. Further to this, he attempted to ostracise me from one person I had respectfully known for many years.

I should have realised what he might do to damage my reputation, as this also happened some years earlier with this same individual in my group days...

I should know a 'leopard will never change his spots' however; I had always been brought up to forgive and forget - but sadly this did not have any affect and to the best of my knowledge he has upset other people with his jealous overtones and similar actions.

Rant over! As this really is not my style...

CHAPTER SIXTEEN

COUNTRY MUSIC INFLUENCES

I began to take an interest in performing country music. I had come to realise that the UK had its own following throughout the British Isles. From a monthly music magazine entitled 'Cross Country' I was able to establish contacts, venues and venue concert bookers.

My own repertoire did consist of a good many, country songs, but having attended one or two shows to gain an insight, I decided I needed to feature not only the older country music (which sometimes gave you the impression it was "Dead Dogs and Verandas") and indeed modern country by the likes of Vince Gill, George Strait/Alan Jackson mould which gave way to fantastic harmonies and very melodic tunes.

I furthered my interest by taking two trips to Nashville, Tennessee. To find more about what makes country tick. I bought many CD'S and commenced to rehearse my set. I was lucky enough to cross 'the pond' to see the American Country Music Awards in 2006 and again in 2009 at the Gaylord/Sonnet centre, Nashville, Tennessee. I took on much work here in the UK which by and large was very well received.

In this country it appears that two types of country music are acceptable.

1. The sit down and listen, or;
2. The Line Dancers.

Well take it from me, the listeners do not like the dancers and vice versa.

So not unexpectedly, some clubs have listeners, and some are for line dancers - but never the twain shall meet - except on rare occasions when insults start to fly around the floor at each other when a mix of un acceptable are present.

Fees on entry generally are modest as clubs in the UK tend to be self-organised and they rely on small door fees, raffles and 'bus stops' to pay the artistes. The amount of work at that time at the turn of the millennium going forward was plentiful, but achieving good fees was always more difficult even though cost of living was continually on the rise.

Me at a Country Music Venue

Travelling to get a full diary was always an issue but by and large the North East provided me with great opportunities. In general nothing at all to do with the Nashville scene but a clique of country organisers over here organise each year a **UK COUNTRY MUSIC AWARDS NIGHT**. This is what happens to the **USA** country music in Nashville of course each November.

Now in my opinion, the UK awards feature more or less the same artistes year on year, the event is nowhere near as lavish as the Nashville event.

If you are in the 'clique' you may get an invite. It is stage managed with a large helping of nepotism sadly. However, for many artistes it is work and for country music lovers to attend shows, costs a fraction what it would be to visit Nashville.

The next phase and opportunity that came my way, was a telephone call from John of Nashville Promotions in Newtownards, County Down in Northern Ireland. He wanted me as part of a tour of British Legion Clubs in Northern Ireland for a weeklong run.

We organised details that come September 2010 I would fly from Liverpool to Aldergrove International airport on the Sunday afternoon. Having landed, I was definitely the last to find my luggage plus my guitar of course and everyone on the flight had already departed. I came through customs and thankfully John and his wife Ann met me, and we swopped pleasantries on the way back in the car.

I stayed with John and Ann throughout the week and was very happy with their hospitality, warmth and kindness towards me. The shows were in a different league to the rest of the UK in that from 8pm until 1pm it was nonstop dancing to the artistes of which no less than 5 acts per night entertained the good people of the emerald isle.

Although I had expected to be playing country music it was the Roy Orbison set that mostly interested the Promoter. So I slipped into that mode and the whole tour was a resounding success. It was like turning the clock back some 30 years with this format, the excitement off the crowds and how life was then in the North of England.

They had even laid a limousine to take me to the first venue which was Gilford British Legion club and an interview and photograph by the local press in making my debut in Northern Ireland. We shared good times that tour and on the bill for the week included the fantastic

Heggarty Twins and Ian McFarlane both big names in Northern Ireland.

Other venues included Belfast British Legion club, Newtownards British Legion Club, Gilford British Legion club, Downpatrick British Legion Club and Enniskillen British Legion Club - all in all, a great experience. I have always wanted a return trip but sadly it never materialised due to various reasons that were too difficult to overcome.

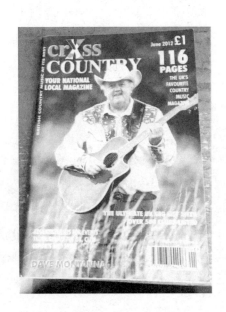

CHAPTER SEVENTEEN

A NIGHT WITH THE STARS

It was a short time later that I became a part of 'A Night with The Stars' show encompassing Roy Orbison/Barry Gibb/Frankie Valli and Del Shannon tribute touring show. This experience changed my outlook and I soon realised that working with Mark Barrie was a whole new experience.

We put a show together with the delightful Penny (Mark's partner) contributing in a big way to produce the show with excellent sound and lighting to make this a nonstop 2-hour spectacular whenever needed. It goes to say that the standard from production, to dress and to presentation, gave a massive uplift to all our performances.

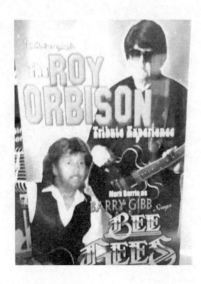

Me as The Roy Orbison Tribute Experience &

Mark Barrie as Barry Gibb

I re utilised some of my previous promoting aspects, by dealing with my network of contacts in venues both in theatres and corporates, to set up some lucrative dates. Mark too had a fair number of decent contacts and we found ourself working a great deal in the Greater Manchester region. We travelled far and wide from Carlisle to Birmingham and Stoke to Whitby with mainly corporates and theatres being our main source of work.

'A Night with the Stars' worked a short summer season in 2017 at Filey Evron Centre for Phil Armitage which ran across the summer months every other Friday. Mark unfortunately developed bile reflux into the throat, leaving a burning sensation and making it impossible to work. The most annoying thing about this problem is that it appears to be no given time when this will occur. So without treatment until it clears, it is not easy to decide when to resume working again.

Mark to my knowledge has had these health issues now for around 10 years or so. This to date, has been one of the areas Mark has had to cancel several times over the past 10 years or so. As I write this issue has not been resolved and we are not sure if it ever will. We can only hope!

We keep in touch from time to time, but the wait is for Mark to decide if a future will be still around over the coming months. It is not functional to arrange series of dates for shows when a cancellation after cancellation then occurs.

So at this stage, a future is not looking rosy and as my years advance and the enforced period of being unable to work due to the Covid pandemic, matters are very much in abeyance. Following the above comments, it seems a matter of time before Mark decides his illness will cause his retirement from the business as he faces some very costly procedures, and the medical findings seem to be reported as inconclusive in a recent letter from him to our road manager David Bell.

With the above I have in the meantime taken on work solo as a Roy Orbison tribute and have worked all over the UK for many periods. My main contact for work - Scott Jordan in Kent has provided me with some wonderful opportunities and am so thankful for their help. The pandemic has made me realise that to continue as a Tribute Artist will not go ahead for so many reasons.

Clubs and pubs are not a suitable environment as punters just turn up for a drink and natter and the artist is not the main consideration. Having worked many theatres and corporates it has decided me to stop while I am at my best vocally and continue my work back of house, when I am able to offer my work experiences and to deal with artists and crew alike, in an area I am most comfortable with.

CHAPTER EIGHTEEN
DRIVING EAST

Backwards the glorious eighties and during 1986 I met up but cannot remember the way I met him but a new acquaintance by the name of Glenn Edson. Glenn being a very genial individual and very comical but a very good guitarist and vocally not unlike the fabulous Bob Dylan.

Glenn was working with a well-known local female vocalist Dawn in a duo under the name 'Tis Woz' the a name change as the duo 'Shoestring'. Now why Shoestring?

It was because Glenn had the facial looks of the TV character Eddie Shoestring at that time. As a duo they were extremely good, and I joined up with them playing bass guitar and the relationship went well into the mid-nineties. We played many gigs, RAF camps and the like. Glenn had some excellent one liner jokes.

He would say 'Anyone from Scotland?' The audience would react, and Glenn would say, 'Your Bus Has just gone!' At the end of the night he would say, 'If you have been drinking and driving don't spill any' and 'If you swerve to avoid a child - don't fall out of bed!' Great character.

Glenn lived quite a solitary life and preferred it that way, so we generally accepted his foibles, as most of us have them. I don't believe Glenn ever had a full-time job but hey-ho maybe that's not such a bad thing. He has survived. I do believe he missed his mum and certainly his dad who was a big influence and followed in his footsteps and ran the weather station they set up in his back garden. He has a son who was living in Scotland when I last made contact, which was a while back now. I always had time for Glenn, as I believe he too has had for me. A very genial and very likeable person.

A particular funny incident... well maybe not so funny, was as a duo we worked a regular Thursday night at Darley's Arms, Porter Street in Hull, a gig we did for Charlie the landlord. Well, one night we were setting up and Glenn had plugged a lead into the amplifier and passed the wire onto me to eventually plug into the speaker. I could see a framed picture near me and thought what a great idea if I pass the wire along the speaker for support. There was a woman sat directly underneath where I was operating, and lo and behold the picture fell and right onto the back of the woman's head! It was hard not to laugh; Glenn went behind the corner as he was killing himself in stitches. I kept a straight face and asked the woman if she was ok.

Having set up our equipment I thought I had better have another word with the lady, but she had disappeared! To this day I do not know if she was ok or not as it was a pretty nasty whack!

Another funny gag was, 'How do you make your own Anti-freeze? Shove her knickers in the fridge.' another one of Glenn's one liners.

From Left: Me, Hugh & Glenn

CHAPTER NINETEEN

EVENTUALLY DRIVING EAST!

My Brother-In-Law Phil Anderson knew Hugh Whitaker's (of Housemartins fame) Mum Vera through working with her at the Hull University.

It was the time in the early nineties when Hugh had earlier in the late 80's left the Housemartins band after scoring some great success with the Housemartins band who had hit songs such as, 'Caravan of Love', 'Build', 'Think For A Minute' and 'Happy Hour'.

Now, Hugh had been working with a local outfit the Penny Candles but was open to doing shows with Glenn and me. We all played instruments, could all sing and we all had much experience in the business.

Hugh was a terrific drummer and could harmonise as I can myself. So with Glenn taking most lead songs and Hugh and I made up with harmony lines, and three part in harmony is really a magical sound for me. We tried with limited success to put in a good selection of Housemartins songs as this was such a great selling point for the venues and to agents and promoters alike. Hugh was never enthused about singing the old hits, but he was so recognisable we simply had to include what we could. We always finished the set up with 'Happy Hour' which was always demanded by the enthusiastic crowds.

Phil my brother-in-Law organised a short tour of Lincolnshire and Leicestershire and we had many a good night along the way. Between the gigs Julie and I decided to get married. Both our parents married co-incidentally on 16 March, different years of course! So having seen that in 1991 the 16 March fell on a Saturday I suggested that it would be an appropriate date to mark on the calendar and tie the knot!

It was arranged and at the Hull Register Office we each invited our own relatives and friends, in fact my mum retorted you've invited them all and....they are all coming!!

We visited to meet the audience performance and reaction. We had a lovely reception at Pearson Institute Club and as entertainment both Glenn and Hugh were happy to give their time and we played a set through the afternoon until it was time to depart to take the train down to London to stay at a lovely hotel in the West End for a few days honeymoon.

It was a lovely time and then back to the real world! As Driving East, we played many gigs, many selling out All over the North and the Midlands and a mention of a regular slot at Immingham De Kyme Hotel in which we played 2 or 3 times a month.

A great following enthused our sets and in between - Hugh played with the 'Penny Candles' group back in Hull. Hugh was a genial and a very laid-back character. Lovely to be in the company of, but often when I went to pick him up he would say, 'I'm just making some tea and toast and not even ready!' I said, 'Great Hugh, but we are due at a venue in the next hour or so.' and with a mug of tea and some toast we would set off.

Happening on more than one occasion – we would break suddenly at the lights in the van, the mug of tea shot off at right angles covering me with tea residue and the toast went flying off into the back of the transit van. Great fun though and many, many laughs!

One night we were playing a Tuesday gig at The Ship, Ann Watson Street in Hull. I saw an axe in the back of Hugh's vehicle. I enquired what that was there for and a few days later the mystery of that came to light.

Now, Hugh had over a period of time earned some good money from the Housemartins days and had bought a house in north Hull. He had let it out to one of his friends and the story closes as follows...

Hugh unfortunately had an altercation due to a private arrangement that backfired with a friend, which resulted in his incarceration for a 2-year period. When the incident occurred, we did visit him in the local nick and all he could do was apologise and tell us he had let everyone down.

Obviously, it weighed on him to have to take drastic action and as always, there was another side to the story of course.

However, Hugh made exceptional progress whilst away and was released at an early stage and spent his new life living in the West Riding by police insistence. Because of this I did lose touch with him as Glenn did too. We did have a get together to see if a reformation might take place, when he eventually returned, Hugh decided against this and by and large all three of us we have not seen each other for some years now. A pity in many ways, as we had some superb nights working together in the late 1980's.

That was many years ago now, and I now believe Hugh is residing back in Hull, but Glenn 's whereabouts is not so clear, but it is an ambition of mine to track him down at some point for a get together.

Well, as years go on phases in lifestyles change and a new direction beckons as with myself. People often asked why we called ourselves Driving East? The straightforward answer was that on every out-of-town show - we were always 'Driving East' back home!

An unfortunate occurrence came on a New Year's Eve performance at Reckitt's Pavilion in Hull. Having unpacked our equipment and having brought our other halves with us, we were told they could not stay as it was New Year's Eve and the people had all bought tickets, and it was out of the question that they could remain. In no way was it ever passed onto us prior that we could not bring guests. Guests at all venues was never an issue. Firstly, because artistes are always granted a guest list, secondly it brought revenue into the venue and to be turned down on a special occasion as this was without a moment's notice was to us an unacceptable measure that the committee had taken at a moment's notice.

So, we stated to the them if we cannot bring our guests in, then we will pack our equipment away and go home to enjoy the evening with better company than we obviously had found at this event. It went on, backwards and forwards and in the end the committee came back and said we can place our guests in a different room which we very politely turned down. We stated it was our New Year's Eve too.

So, after a while we saw a turnaround by the committee and our guests were given a 'pokey' area well away from our performance area which we accepted as they had seen our act many times before. The point of our concern was no one had bothered to contact us from the organisers to inform us that our guests were not invited! If they had, we would have turned the gig down anyway.

An amusing note, one New Year's Eve in that we were booked at the local Inglemire club one particular occasion... Now this club was literally a 200 yards walk from where we lived. Julie put the turkey in the oven just before we went to the gig and halfway through, she returned to our house to turn the turkey and then returned to the club to continue watching the show. What a multi-tasker! I had the pleasure of closing several venues during my musical career, including the Hull Holy Name social club. (Which is now a care home.)

In short, I was the final artiste to grace the stage of this social club venue. One of my early contemporaries Johnny Brown attended this last show and it was a pleasure to meet up again after such a long absence. In the late 70's I gigged with John working country venues such as the Humber Keel in Beverley every other Tuesday with John and working the alternate Tuesday at Driffield Buck Hotel.

We had some great times in Driffield and definitely had a fan base which grew, and we played to a packed house on most nights. At Driffield we were usually joined by Dave Christian (real name Ron Bowden) Dave was great vocalist and shone on many of the high registered songs such as Wimoweh, in Dreams and the like. Years later on a rather sadder note, in 2006 I was working a disco show at the Merchant Navy Hotel in Hull and sat in a corner was Dave - I noticed while I was setting up. We then spent a good half hour reliving past times.

Dave lived in a flat local to the hostelry. I did my show and the next day departed for Madeira for a two-week holiday. On my return I found out very sadly that Dave had passed away that very evening in his flat. By the time I was given this information, the funeral had already happened, so I was even more gutted and often think about the good times we had. Dave was a real genial guy and I was so sorry to hear of his demise and the timing which I found to this day was really eerie. Dave was a part of a great duo in the 1960's working venues as The Serenades. He sang his Roy Orbison songs in a particular special way.

CHAPTER TWENTY

THE CHANTRY

A handful of years back we had the pleasure of making contact with Jimmy Patton. As a family my two boys Gareth and Scott were taken to see the Chuckle Brothers who performed annual pantomimes and toured with Chuckle Vision. The main cast being Paul and Barry Chuckle and Jimmy and Brian Patton.

All of course were family related. Jimmy and Brian Patton were the eldest and Paul and Barry were the youngest of the brothers. Meeting by chance and speaking with Jimmy, he told us about a weekly get together of artistes at the Chantry Hotel in Dronfield hosted by Roy and Jackie Toaduff themselves in their time, a fantastic song and dance act who had worked all over the world. He told me they always commenced for breakfast in the conservatory and many artistes attended if they were available, names such as Bernie Clifton, Bobby Knutt, and we as a family including Julie and son Scott often had the pleasure of meeting Bobby Dennis world renowned comedian and singer.

Jimmy Patton of Chuckle Vision fame organised a film quiz, Bobby Dennis who was often slaughtered by Bernie Clifton with his own quiz and so many laughs it was usually uncontrollable. Terry Herrington, fabulous pianist backed any artiste willing to give a voice in the music room so in between 10am and 2pm so much fun was had by all concerned.

It was ideal for myself, Julie and Scott as most times we went by train and the station was two minutes from the hotel. We had many, many Thursdays at this place just full of wonderful people. Bernie Clifton and Bobby Dennis as aforementioned almost worked as a double act throughout so it was entertainment at a premium free of charge! A major guest for me was the irrepressible one and only Howard Copley.

Howard was a retiring journalist with, 'The local rag 'The Mercury' and without a doubt he is a comedian in his own right! I forged a link with Howard and class him very high in my list of likeable talented people I am privileged to know.

My son Scott, Bernie Clifton, David Bell and
Julie, my wife.

At the age of approaching mid-seventies, I do find however, travel a little more wearing and life is definitely much harder to bear with aches and pains you never knew existed in earlier life.

Fun & Frolics at The Chantry with Howard Copley, Scott, Jean Harrison and Bernie Clifton.

To travel and then do a gig on an average round trip of 200 miles, then drive straight home is - with age, becoming a strain. Although my overall health is ok, apart from diabetes of which I must take an array of tablets and a weekly injection - which without doubt has enhanced my lifestyle... My good friend David Bell who was our roadie for several years when I worked, 'The Night With The Stars Show' unfortunately he too has had illness issues and long journeys are not in his vocabulary now either and understandably.

Mark the other half of the, 'Night with The Stars' show has suffered vocal wise for 12 years to my knowledge, and wisely he is looking at the medical side for now, but to hopefully one day be able to re commence doing something musically.

Back to Dave who is a natural comedian in his own right and he often opened our shows with his ventriloquist doll Isaac.

The surname of his doll was 'Hunt' but we had better not go down that road... David himself being ex RAF and a Policeman has always had some funny tales and anecdotes to tell. An extrovert in dress and a wonderful sense of humour, liked by all who know him. David by his own admission is everyone's friend and does not like to rock the boat. He has for me been a good friend over the many years and will drive you anywhere at any time.

Like his dad Harry, he has always had a wicked sense of humour and to this day we keep in touch on a regular basis. David has so many friends, he tends to flit from person to person and it depends really for his social life who is his 'flavour of the month' - having said that, what great company it is to be with Dave. Today and more than enough reason down to the pandemic my live shows were curtailed for 18 months.

I had the pleasure in August 2021 of fronting a Festival at Hull's East Park with my Roy Orbison tribute. My wife, youngest son and my Mother-In-Law sat behind the stage and heard me, electing not to see me as well, they knew what I looked like anyway I suppose. Dave Bell made his usual appearance and the thinking that in his words too he thought that it was a remarkably good performance, his words as I always fail to recognise what is good or not so good performance wise although the excellent sound system in place made life so much easier that afternoon. A private gig in Sheffield followed in September, but to date I have not gigged at all since then.

I have half promised (if I am able) to do a pensioners do at my Mother-In-Law's Haven of Rest in June 2022. Pensioners - well I am one too!

This event, I can confirm was achieved, albeit the day turned out to be wet and miserable, but we still managed a set between the raindrops, with the proceeds all going to the Royal British Legion.

It was great to see everyone at the Haven attending including Drypool Lil, Joyce with her Egyptian musical sketch and fab to meet up again with the excellent Ray Wardell a top entertainer in the true sense of the word, who delighted the audience with some songs and humour too.

Currently for interest I spend much time working at the Hull Bonus Arena and York Barbican and shortly too at the Hull City Hall and Hull New Theatre. All the staff at all of the venues are now all my good friends, including all the management. A wonderful opportunity where I do meet many likeminded show-business people on a regular basis, covering dressing room areas mainly when I attend for a working shift at the Bonus arena.

I love the work, adore the staff and we have many amusing moments together whilst diligently working. It is always good to speak to some of the appearing artistes at the arena should they wish to. In recent times, we had Paul Heaton and an interesting few minutes relating to taking the walk to the stage. From the dressing rooms on level 1 all the artistes have the choice of entrance to the stage by either taking the lift or using the stairs which is by far the longer way.

However, Paul through his Promoter indicated that he would not use the lift going into the arena in case it malfunctioned, and he was aware that an arena full of expectant fans could be left wanting, if this was to happen. So his philosophy was to take the stairs and after the show take the lift upwards and only then take his chances. Others such as Mick Hucknall have also taken up this same idea. As the gag goes, 'I was once a lift attendant, but I resigned as there were too many Ups and Downs.'

As I stated, I am about to embark on another role in entertainment by working casually also at the Hull City Hall and Hull New Theatre.

I am looking forward to working with very enterprising and likeable contemporaries and another chapter in my long and illustrious life turns over a new page of hope and destiny.

With work at the Bonus Arena/York Barbican and running side by side with Hull New Theatre and Hull City Hall, I am keeping in touch with the work I enjoy the most, the people and above all the entertainment!

I have recently been set the task of applying for my latest three year stint to continue as an SIA Security (Industry Authority) it involved a full day learning Emergency First Aid procedures followed by an exam, with another 2 days learning about security awareness, further Physical Intervention skills applying them both practically and theory in the exams plus learning and exams on the current and ongoing concerns related to Terrorism threats and possible active use by outside bodies.

This also included a three part written exam. Well, after all that, I did pass and can continue more newly found involvements within events at the place I work in Hull and York at respective stadium and theatres.

More recently, Bryan Adams adorned the Bonus Arena and my estimation to him went sky high as he and his band took to the stage to work a two hours and ten minutes nonstop entertaining set without an interval. His set was flawless, and the crowd went really wild. Bryan spent the waiting before the show time talking and mingling with many people backstage. Another interesting visit to the Hull Bonus Arena being the Pet Shop Boys and even though this outfit have adorned many a worldwide stage it was the first ever visit to Hull. It was a pleasure to see, meet and spend a few minutes with the boys who gave a rapturous audience a most scintillating performance and they too said it was the best reaction they had encountered on the UK tour and looked forward to putting Hull on their next concert calendar.

During their stay the Boys had a tour of the city, thoroughly enjoying for them an untapped area of interest.

Throughout the year 2022, I have re visited York Barbican to work some interesting shifts since the ending of the pandemic. One particular one was the Jeff Beck concert which actually featured Johnny Depp the actor of 'Pirates Of The Caribbean' fame. Now one of Jeff's close friends is Johnny who halfway through Jeff's set came onto the stage, playing guitar and singing and talking to the crowd. Because of his name being linked with a major court case in America his profile had been to the fore and excitement at his appearance at the Barbican had reached 'fever pitch'. I had the distinction of relieving a 'dressed up' Jack Sparrow his sword, his dagger and his gun. Box office charge £2 per item so this guy was minus £6 before he had even entered the auditorium!

It is a massive no, no to enter a public environment displaying and carrying such equipment!

Dave Orton and Mark Dawson are two legends at the Barbican and they really are acts in their own right and loved by everyone at this popular venue. Mark has two hats he wears 1. As a Security officer and 2. As a supervisor, so beware if you fall foul of the latter! They meet and greet the visiting patrons and is something really special as these two are the epitome of how to be welcoming with all visiting guests. More recently Bryan Adams adorned the Bonus Arena and my estimation to him went sky high as he and his band took to the stage to work a two hours and ten minutes nonstop entertaining set without an interval.

His set was flawless and the crowd went really wild. Bryan spent the waiting before the show time talking and mingling with most people backstage and enjoys singing so much he does his warm ups in view and sound of anyone who was around at the time. Another interesting visit to the Hull Bonus Arena being the Pet Shop Boys and even though this outfit have adorned many a worldwide stage it was the first ever visit to Hull.

It was a pleasure to see, meet and spend a few minutes with the boys who gave a rapturous audience a most scintillating performance and they too said it was the best reaction they had encountered on the UK tour and looked forward to putting Hull on their next concert calendar. During their stay the Boys had a tour of the city,

thoroughly enjoying for them an untapped area
of interest.

THE LAST WORD

In my family life now our youngest son Scott, is a member of Barton Inclusive Football team which caters for individuals with either learning difficulties, special needs and some of a physical nature. Scott, although he has right sided hemiplegia (lack of normal use of right side of the body) not only reads the game well but has good left foot ability and has been in the side that recently won the South Yorkshire Abilities League and Cup gaining man of the match that won the trophy for his team during 2022.

My eldest Gareth recently married Emma. Emma hails from Salford and they are now both qualified Lawyers and overall are such a credit to our family. Ironically, they met on the first day at the University of Law, reportedly in the lift! The University of Law now employ my son as a tutor!

Gareth too spent his teen years footballing wise representing Hull Schoolboys at under 15 level and locally with Hessle Sporting club under the watchful eye of Charlie Walker, then onto Scarborough AFC and finally Leeds United where he played in the same under 16 team with the likes of Fabian Delph who has been a pro footballer for many years and recently announced his retirement.

Gareth unfortunately broke a finger diving at the feet of a Doncaster Rovers player at that time and eventually had to have an operation on one of his fingers. This made his mind up that as a goalkeeper and his upward growth diminishing, his love of playing the piano and violin, it was time to take a sensible decision on his ambitions footballing wise, to move into safer waters and onwards and upwards, career wise as well.

Gareth and Scotty are model sons who have brought only pleasure.

My life still continues, 'my eyesight is failing, I keep running into pubs!' - and I feel that at this point in life, I have been able to fulfil my family's wishes and call a halt to this manuscript and trust that each and every one of you that reads my memoir, find they have been able to learn, understand and above all - enjoy this continuing story which has been hectic at times, but so life rewarding and in parts hopefully amusing.

Me and my Wife, Julie in Malta, 1988

LIFE HAS BEEN AN ADVENTURE
SUPPOSE YOU COULD SAY THAT'S TRUE
BUT YOU-HAVE WORKED VERY HARD
IN ALL THE JOBS YOU HAD TO DO

TRIED YOUR HAND AT MANY THINGS
ENJOYED BEING YOUR OWN BOSS
OWNING DIFFERENT ESTABLISHMENTS
SELLING NEWSPAPERS FROM 4 SHOPS

YOU QUALIFIED AS A REFEREE
YOUR DEDICATION YOU COULD NOT
FALTER
EVEN REFEREED A GAME AT WEMBLEY
AND TOOK CHARGE OF A MATCH IN MALTA

BUT PERFORMING HAS BEEN YOUR FORTE
YOUR SINGING IS REALLY GREAT
AS ROY ORBISON, THE MAN IN BLACK
YOUR TRIBUTE SHOW'S FIRST RATE

ENTERTAINING ALL AROUND THE WORLD
LOCALLY WITH BANDS AND DUO'S TOO
TO QUOTE "IT'S BEEN SO FULLFILLING"
HOPE YOU KNOW WE ARE PROUD OF YOU

SO YES, IT'S BEEN AN ADVENTURE
AND THE YEARS HAVE GONE BY SO FAST
BUT LOOKING BACK ON REFLECTION
IT'S REALLY BEEN QUITE A BLAST!

Poem written by my Wife, Julie

ACKNOWLEDGEMENTS

Firstly, I would like to thank above all Julie my wonderful and loyal wife. Howard my dearest brother for his lifelong support and friendship, Sue my sister in law and family, our wonderful sons Gareth and Scott for whom I am so proud of for many, many reasons.

To the extended family, my dear Mother-In-Law Valerie, the late Dennis a truly clever and wonderful man, Dear Emma my sister-in-law, Phil my well respected brother in law, charming Abigail my sister in law and family. A massive thank you to Florence, and the team at P & P Publishing who liked my manuscript and helped me to 'put the baby to bed', in readiness for the typesetting of this anthology.

To David Gordon Bell a lifelong friend, for providing some back in the years photos, which help illustrate this book and recalling memorable moments and for his excellent and memorable moments along the way. To Geoff Todd my dear cousin who kindly wrote the foreword. To my daughter Hayley Gibbs and my son Jonathan

David Orriss both sadly missing from my life, but lovely childhood memories.

THANK YOU TO ALL that have enriched my life passed, and present, with support that have helped me on my chosen pathway and in no particular order as follows:- Valerie & Dennis Anderson, David G.Bell, Mike Mearns, Mark & Penny Scott, Tracey Wilson, Ken and Alan Wilkinson, Mark Dawson, Dave Orton, Graham & Pat Roberts, Arthur Clinton, Fred and Kitty Orriss, Andrew, Carla & Matthew Orriss, Geoff and Shirley Todd, Stan and Pat Todd, Elsie and Stan Cole, Margaret and Arthur Holliday, Peter and Katherine Wheldale, John and Edith Wheldale, Pauline and Jim Goldspink, Bobby Brown, Phil Hough, Bronwyn Walker, Matt Carrington, Les Cammish, Ron Hunt, Chris Bell, Ian P Bell, Sophie James, Tony Normington, Steve Bruce, John Hawley, Justin Whittle, Wally Jude, Tom Wilson, Brian, Harry & Molly Chapman, Dave & Marianne Stones, Bill Chester, Bobby Knutt, Howard Copley, Ian Gray, Don Holden, Tim Myers, Pete McCleod, Stuart Sorrie, Tex Milne, Rev R.W. Dallas, Jimmy & Brian Patton, Paul & Barry Elliott (Chuckle Brothers), Vic Savile, Roy Uzzell, Clemente Cattini, Roy & Jackie Toaduff, Terry

Herrington, Paul Daniels, Jack Meddings, Ian Ogden, Michael & Andrew Baitson, David Chick, Carol Peak, Mike Carter, Janet Barley, Joanne Barley, Albert Barley, Fred Barley, Mick Ronson, Danny Walters, Stan Robinson, Phil Parkman, Liz Hugill, Jeff Wilson, Chris Nagy, Alan Young, Pete and Denise Loft, Mike Peterson, Bert Peterson, Mike Wright, Barry & Janet Donald, Alan & Jackie Donald, Robert McLeish Jnr, Florence Hannath, Peter Groves, Dick Ray, Billy Forrest, Glenn Edson, Hugh Whitaker, Bernie Clifton, Trevor Sylvester, Mark Conrad, Steve Wray, John & Margaret Windass, Dean Windass, John Oxley, Paul & Aelish Anderson, Doreen Fines, Tex Milne, Tim Beaumont, John Wagstaff, Sammy King, Dave Wright, Jean Harrison, Pat Haynes, Dave Newstone, Les Turner, Peter Bacon, Gordon Suddaby, Chloe Atkinson, Heidi Sadler, Sam Ryder, Dan Harris, Tommy Bruce, Peter Wallis, Bob Storry, Harry Braimbridge, Wally Garfitt, Lisa Garfitt, Alison Bache, Jim Bache, Jason & Janet Bache, Alison Fewster, Dick Walker, Barry Richards, Gary Nicholson, Barry Edwards, Mikey North, Ray Quinn, Matthew Wolfenden, Kim, Steve at Scott Jordan Entertainments, Janelle and Darran, Ben, Chloe & Kieran Taylor, Ann, Kelsey & Jo/ Steve Bond, Dave Cooper,

Jacqui Pym, Ron Dawes, Ken & Peter Newington, Phil Wyvill-Bell, Mike Aramayo, Frank Broughton, Jack Tarr, Tony Youngs, Yuleo, Mary Steadman, Roger & Judy Gibson, Tony Munzer, Martin Bremner, Chris Rimmington, Geoff Johnson, Gareth Griffiths, Carrick Anderson, Darren Moore, Paul Dearing, Kevin Williams, Roy Farnill, Jim Tiplady, Jane Jacklin, John Hill, Dean Cummings, Tracey Wilson, John and Iris Brown, Barry Johns, Roy Uzzell, Dave Lofthouse, Phil and Abigail Anderson